THE GREAT PHYSICIAN

Still on call

THE GREAT PHYSICIAN

Still on call

A BOOK ON HEALING
BY EVELYN GIPSON

This edition published in 2016 by Great Big Life Publishing
Empower Centre, 83-87 Kingston Road, Portsmouth, PO2 7DX, UK.

British Library Cataloguing in Publication Data

A catalogue record for this book is available from the British Library

Unless otherwise marked scripture quotations are taken from the Holy Bible, King James Version.
Scripture quotations marked 'NKJV' are taken from the New King James Version®. Copyright © 1982 by Thomas Nelson. Used by permission. All rights reserved.
Scripture quotations marked 'AMP' are taken from the Amplified® Bible (Classic Edition). Copyright © 1954, 1958, 1962, 1964, 1965, 1987 by The Lockman Foundation. Used by permission. www. Lockman.org
Scripture quotations marked 'NLT' are taken from Holy Bible, New Living Translation, copyright © 1996, 2004, 2015 by Tyndale House Foundation. Used by permission of Tyndale House Publishers Inc., Carol Stream, Illinois 60188. All rights reserved.
Scripture quotations marked 'NIV' are taken from The Holy Bible, New International Version®, Copyright © 1973, 1978, 1984, 2011 by Biblica, Inc.® Used by permission. All rights reserved worldwide.
Scripture quotations marked 'TLB' are taken from The Living Bible. Copyright © 1971 by Tyndale House Foundation. Used by permission of Tyndale House Publishers Inc., Carol Stream, Illinois 60188. All rights reserved.
Scripture quotations marked 'GW' are taken from GOD'S WORD®, © 1995 God's Word to the Nations. Used by permission of Baker Publishing Group.

PRINT: ISBN 978-0-9932693-8-7
EBOOK: ISBN 978-0-9932693-9-4

AUTHOR'S STATEMENT

'The Word of God is Truth.'

The Word says, 'By Jesus' stripes we are healed' (1 Peter 2:24). You either believe the Bible or you don't. It does you absolutely no good to believe in half truths or mix in any other belief systems with your faith. The Word of God is the final say and has the final say. Operating in absolute surrender to the Lord is the foundation of faith.

INTENT AND PURPOSE

The purpose of this book is to impart some of the knowledge I have gained during my lifetime study on the subject of healing. Healing is a portion of what Jesus appropriated for us on the cross. This book has been created to give you some understanding on how to receive your healing, how to walk in your healing, and how to maintain and protect your healing. My heartfelt intent is that this book will inspire you to seek the knowledge of God in the area of healing and train you to pursue healing for yourself as well as for others. Make it a point to diligently study the scriptures within as a launching pad to unlock the mystery of God, especially where healing is concerned.

CONTENTS

DEDICATION

My heart belongs to Jesus, Who is the Savior of my soul
He gave His life to prove His love to see that I'm made whole.
He who knew no sin became all sin that I might be set free
He took the blame, He took the shame, He did all that for me.

That would have been enough, you see, to save my soul from Hell
But He did so much more than that, to make sure that I am well.
He took the stripes upon His back, all thirty-nine you see,
That was done to pay for all my pain and misery.

He loves me and no matter what, He meant that I should live
in freedom from all death and hell that the enemy could give.
I now accept all that He took that day upon the Tree
So I will praise Him all my life throughout eternity.

Such a Savior who could find that would prove His love like that
He gave His life, His blood, His wealth, He even gave His sweat.
He paid the price for every sin, the curse removed forever
The Son of God came down to man and from man's sins delivered.

If that was all my Savior did, I'd be forever grateful
He was all God, all man, sinless and was completely faithful.
He paid the price for all mankind, left nothing here undone
Redeemed us from the total curse, we're freed from every one.

Just enter into what He gave
Abundant life so free.
Be saved, be healed, it's all been paid
He bought us liberty.

FOREWORD

How does one write about a hero in their life and convince the reader that has never met the hero that it is all true? That is the way I feel about Evelyn Gipson. How do I convince you that this woman of God is not only who she says she is, and knows what she says she knows, but is even more?

I have known Evelyn for over twenty years. In the beginning she was a mythical spiritual giant. I had heard about healings and extraordinary encounters where she would lead complete strangers to the Lord in the most random places. Stories of people being set free from spiritual oppression, and stories of this fiery red headed woman storming into hospitals, nursing homes and homeless shelters bringing God's word and power into the lives of hundreds and maybe even thousands.

As I have watched her over these decades, I have more then realized that this is not a mythical or fictional exaggerated character, but a real and genuine woman of God. She is the book of Acts with skin on. Some might think with Evelyn's testimonies, experiences and anointing that she might be self-absorbed, proud, and maybe even aloof towards the average person. The truth is that she is the most humble, loving, and authentic person you could ever meet. Her years of walking with God have made her more like the real Jesus than the stained glass window version. She is a friend of hurting sinners as well as struggling believers, going the extra mile to save a heart for eternity or heal a body so that they can have a few more years with their families and finish their earthly destiny. I also appreciate that after burying people we were praying for; that she never quits believing or praying for the next one. You see, God does heal, God has promised healing, and we have seen countless healings, but sometimes people die even though you have done all you know to do. It is in such a moment that some throw in the towel. Evelyn chooses to use these moments as fuel for the fire. She continues on, declaring in her heart that we won't lose the next one.

This book will bless you because it not only carries Evelyn's wisdom, but also her spirit. If you listen, you will hear her heart beating with purpose to heal the sick. She never sought healing to make her name great, but rather to help hurting people and give God all the praise along the way. You will feel love pour through and hopefully catch her compassion, zeal and determination. Perhaps you too will refuse to quit believing and praying for miracles in this generation. I know you will learn a lot and use this book as a resource. Read it like a student, but also read it as one being mentored by a modern day healing evangelist and apostle of faith.

Kevin Kringel
Lead Pastor, Life Church

INTRODUCTION

My husband Roy and I were saved in a small Baptist church in November of 1967, and just one week later I was asked to be a part of the Children's ministry. I learned a lot from the six-year-olds in those Sunday school classes, and I've never stopped learning what God has tried to teach me. I spent a lot of time in those early years studying the foundational teachings of strong men and women of God like Kenneth E. Hagin, Oral Roberts, Kenneth Copeland, and Marilyn Hickey.

Unfortunately, that little church didn't believe in any of the spiritual gifts. They thought healing, and all the other gifts, passed away with the last apostle. As I began to read and study the Word of God, some of the things I found didn't line up with what the church taught.

I was healed from a blood disease by what I like to call a 'faith accident'. I went to God and told Him that my church said He didn't heal anymore, and that if I was a bother to Him, I was sorry. I said, 'When I read the Word, it seems to me that You are still healing people.' I continued, 'If You *are* still healing people, and I am not being presumptuous, would You please heal me?' That is just what He did! That got me into trouble with my church and when I was filled with the Holy Spirit in 1972, I was in even more trouble!

We left the church with the strong push of religion at our backs and went to an Assemblies of God church in Rockford, Illinois, where we stayed for thirty years. Eleven years ago God released us from that church and sent us to Life Church in Roscoe, Illinois.

My deepest desire has always been to be pleasing to God. I want to be in the center of His will and don't mind bucking the mainstream if He shows me something in His Word. I have been teaching healing and seeing God heal for forty-nine years. I am amazed by His grace and compassion and still gasp at the fact that He would see fit to use me. I will never stop being astounded that He chose me and is allowing me to serve Him and encourage others to serve Him.

I have seen many saved as God has opened doors for me to share Jesus. Years ago they used to tell me that people over the age of fifty didn't get saved; their hearts were too hardened. Maybe it is an 'end time' thing, but God has allowed me to lead hundreds of people over the age of seventy-five to the saving knowledge of Jesus, and has allowed me to be an instrument in seeing thousands healed and filled with the Holy Spirit. I will always be grateful for the opportunity to serve Him. I am blessed beyond measure.

God wants to do the same thing with and for you that He did for me. You are not reading this book by accident. Remember this as you read: God always gives you more than you ever ask for.

"Now unto him that is able to do exceeding abundantly above all that we ask or think, according to the power that worketh in us"
(Ephesians 3:20)

Approximately two thousand years ago a decree was issued from the judgment seat of God. It provided legal protection for the church against the devil.

When Jesus died for our sins, the 'ruler of this world' was judged (John 16:11). Our debts were nailed to the cross. When Jesus died, He cancelled the indictment against you; principalities and powers were disarmed.

Because of Jesus we have a legal right not only to be protected from the enemy, but also to triumph over him (Colossians 2:13-14).

The sacrifice of Christ was so complete, and the judicial decision from God against Satan so decisive, that divine protection is enough to cover us, the entire redeemed church from sin, sickness, and defeat.

Everything that needed to be done was done on the cross. Jesus healed you at Calvary. It is a done deal! He doesn't have to come down and touch you, or come down and heal you. He did it all on the day He gave His life on Calvary.

Jesus said in 3 John 2, *"Beloved, I wish above all things that you may prosper and be in health even as your soul prospers."*

Your healing is promised and is a very secure thing. Take hold of what was done for you today and begin to confess it out loud. Tell yourself what God says about you.

It is not so much what you say to others that you believe; it is what you tell yourself.

Chapter 1

INTRODUCTION TO HEALING

B e assured that God wants you to be healthy and well. The Word
is very clear on that.

*"Beloved, I wish above all things that thou mayest prosper and
be in health, even as thy soul prospereth."*
(3 John 2)

*"Who Himself bore our sins in His own body on the tree that we,
having died to sins, might live for righteousness—by whose
stripes you were healed."*
(1 Peter 2:24, NKJV)

*"Surely He has borne our griefs and carried our sorrows; yet
we esteemed Him stricken, smitten by God, and afflicted. But
He was wounded for our transgressions, He was bruised for
our iniquities; the chastisement for our peace was upon Him,
and by His stripes we are healed."*
(Isaiah 53:4-5, NKJV)

Jesus carried out His part of the covenant when He was beaten
before being hung on the cross. He bore the stripes for your healing.

This is a biggie! The blood flowed from those wounds on His back. Your faith in what that blood did for you will produce a manifestation of your healing.

You can establish in your heart that the work concerning your healing has already been done. Jesus completed what was needed to do the job. Now your job is to believe God's Word and to give the Word of God first place in your life. If the Word says do something, then do it. *He did all the giving and we do all the receiving.* Much like you received salvation from sin, you receive what was done at that whipping post. Often we are still waiting for Jesus to come and do something, while He is waiting for us to believe and take hold of what was already done.

After establishing in your heart that God has already done what was needed concerning our healing, we are commanded to walk by faith. So, with simple faith lay hold of your healing. You cannot look around at circumstances, situations, people, or even what has happened to others. Simply study the Word of God until it is so grounded in your heart that nothing can move you off what God has said about you and your healing. Fill yourself so full of God's Word that whenever you get bumped, all that spills out is the Word of God. Granted, that takes some work, but it is necessary if you are going to enjoy healing and divine health in the days in which we live.

If you will do a study in the gospels of who Jesus is, you will realize that Jesus and His Word are one and the same, and it will become much easier for you to receive. When you know who Jesus is, and how much He loves you, you can easily receive from Him whatever it is you need to live life to the fullest.

"In the beginning was the Word, and the Word was with God, and the Word was God."
(John 1:1)

My pastor, Kevin Kringel, shared with us one day that he copied by hand every word from the gospels. He said he always gets revelation out of the Word when he opens the Bible, no matter where he reads. I think I have figured out why. He got to know Jesus and what He is like as he copied the words from Matthew to John. Because Pastor Kevin took the time to write out all that Jesus said, Jesus revealed Himself to him and continues to reveal Himself each and every time he goes into the Word of God.

Let's step back to Genesis 1:26 for just a moment. God gave Adam complete dominion and authority over everything on this planet. When Adam ate of the tree of the knowledge of good and evil, he sold out to the outlaw Satan. All the dominion God had given to Adam now belonged to Satan. God could not make another man because He had given the earth to Adam. The earth was now under the control of Satan, along with the authority originally given to Adam.

The dirt that formed Adam no longer belonged to God, thus God had to find another way to get back the man He so dearly loved. He found a man from Ur of the Chaldees named Abram (later Abraham), a man who would believe God no matter what He asked him to do. Having found such a man, God made a covenant with him. Abraham was a man who believed God (Romans 4:3).

Let me take a moment and explain to you what a covenant is. When two people planned to cut a covenant together, it was a very sacred thing. It was a lasting agreement that could not be broken, and it was made in blood. Most people or tribes would cut a covenant with a tribe who was strong in an area in which they were weak. If you were a farmer but didn't know how to war, you would choose a tribe with strong fighters and persuade them to cut a covenant with you. They would exchange names and pledge to defend and feed one another. They pledged to give all that they had to each other, and if either ever needed anything, they had to provide it or they could be killed.

God asked Abraham to cut a covenant with Him. The problem was that Abraham would not be able to keep his part of the covenant because of man's sin nature, so God caused Abraham to fall into a deep sleep, then Jesus and God the Father pledged the covenant together.

> *"And it came to pass, that, when the sun went down, and it was dark, behold a smoking furnace, and a burning lamp that passed between those pieces."*
> *(Genesis 15:17)*

The smoking furnace was God and the burning lamp was Jesus. It was a covenant that could not be broken. God set it up so that He would have to destroy Himself in order for the agreement to be broken. This was a binding agreement between the Father and the Son.

> *"Whereas this One [Christ], after He had offered a single sacrifice for our sins [that shall avail] for all time, sat down at the right hand of God, then to wait until His enemies should be made a stool beneath His feet. For by a single offering He has forever completely cleansed and perfected those who are consecrated and made holy."*
> *(Hebrews 10:12-14, AMP)*

Through Abraham, God has made a covenant with us, and a part of that covenant is healing and health. Just like salvation from sins, we can do nothing to achieve our healing except to lay hold of what Jesus has done for us. And, like Abraham, we cannot keep the covenant. Our part is to accept Jesus and what He did for us—what was accomplished at the cross—and then lean hard on that knowledge. Jesus has totally fulfilled what God required to free us from the punishment that was due us from the fall of Adam.

> *"For if because of one man's trespass (lapse, offense) death reigned through that one, much more surely will those who*

receive [God's] overflowing grace (unmerited favor) and the free gift of righteousness [putting them into right standing with Himself] reign as kings in life through the one Man Jesus Christ (the Messiah, the Anointed One)."
(Romans 5:17, AMP)

I am convinced that the reason why most people don't receive the manifestation of their healing is a sense of being condemned. When we sin we open the door, much like Adam did when he fell, to Satan who brings condemnation. If you do not realize that Jesus upheld your part of the covenant and that the judgment you deserved came upon Him, then you will either consciously or unconsciously begin to try and pay for it yourself.

I can think of a thousand and one reasons why I should not be healed, but I can only think of ONE reason why I *should* be healed. His name is JESUS. He took my place for my sin and my disease. He redeemed me from the curse of the law (Galatians 3:13).

It is now up to us to receive by faith what was done for us. It has to be a matter of just receiving. Realize that you cannot pay even a small portion of the debt that was owed. Nothing you have done, or could ever hope to do, can pay for what was done for you by the Beloved Son of God. So come in faith and receive full redemption. We need only to throw ourselves on the mercy of God and receive the full portion of what Jesus did for us.

Satan does NOT have the legal right to put on me (or you) what was paid for at the cross by our Savior. I do not have to receive anything from Satan that Christ has redeemed me from. Freedom from the curse belongs to me now, regardless of what I may have done or may not have done, even after my salvation.

I do want to stress, however, that we should endeavor to live a clean life; one free from deliberate, habitual sin. When we sin we give the enemy legal rights; in other words, an open door to our soul (our mind, will, and emotions). This is when trouble comes. Satan is our enemy and will use any and every door left open to destroy you through deception, doubt, and condemnation. Satan is a legalist and will do whatever he can to get into your mind, causing you to stray from the truth of God's Word. Deliberate, unrepentant sin gives him the right to mess with your mind. We do not have to fear him, because he is a defeated foe. BUT Satan is very good at what he does, and he will mess with your thoughts and place you under condemnation. Condemnation clouds your vision to what actually belongs to you. A person may not realize that condemnation is there.

The Bible tells us that God is no respecter of persons. What Jesus did for one, He will do for another. He is not withholding anything from us. It is the way we think that blocks our ability to receive the healing that was provided. We will have to change our thought patterns and begin to believe God in order to receive what was made available for us.

Now let's move forward and see that it is God's will for you to be healed.

> *"My child, pay attention to what I say. Listen carefully to my words. Don't lose sight of them. Let them penetrate deep into your heart, for they bring life to those who find them, and healing to their whole body. Guard your heart above all else, for it determines the course of your life."*
> *(Proverbs 4:20-23, NLT)*

CHAPTER 1 NOTES AND REFLECTIONS

Chapter 2

HEALING IS THE WILL OF GOD

Make the Word of God Your Final Authority

As I've stated previously, a person should decide to make the Word of God the final authority. If you don't believe God's Word and make it the final authority in your life, you may fail in your attempt to receive healing. This is the foundational key to healing.

To make God's Word the final authority means to trust what God says in His Word. We must rest in the promises He made to us in the Word and let go of our doubts. We do this by taking daily, consistent doses of His Word, and making the decision that if God promised it in His Word, we will believe and act on His Word.

I should explain that there are different types of healings. At this time, I am giving you suggestions on receiving healing by faith. There are also miracles, those healings that happen instantly. To receive healing by faith, you must grab on to what the Word says about your healing. Then you must hold on to the truth of God's Word until you see the manifestation of your healing.

Years ago, I was involved in a road traffic accident and rolled my van four times, resulting in my scapula becoming broken. The doctor told me I would have limited use of my arm and that it would mimic an arthritic shoulder with pain when changes in the weather came. I took hold of the Word of God which said, according to Romans 8:11, that my shoulder was quickened and made alive by the Spirit of God which dwelt within me. I began to confess the Word and held fast to the promise until it manifested six weeks later. I didn't have surgery, even though the shoulder was broken, because the x-ray showed that the shoulder had grown together after a few weeks, which the doctor stated was impossible. I now have no pain and unlimited use of my arm.

I took hold of what the Scripture said and did not let go until my complete healing manifested. I didn't ignore what the doctor told me, I just chose to believe another report. That is why I tell you to make the Word of God your *final* authority. If you don't, you will be moved off your promise by doctor's reports, pain, tests, or what other people say. Hold fast to what God has told you in His Word. Don't let go of the promise until what God said you can have shows up in the natural.

If you take what the Word of God says and make that your confession and determine not to be moved by pain, lack of use at the moment, or any other discouragement, you can force the Word to work.

Please note that I am *not* saying you are 'forcing' God; you are instead 'forcing' the system He set in place to work for you. God gave the Israelites the Promised Land, but they had to force the occupants of the land to give it up. Our Promised Land of healing belongs to us, but it may take several battles to possess it. You may have to force the enemy off your property, out of your body. You are enforcing the victory Jesus obtained at the cross. Do not deny the circumstances; instead deny their right to be there.

It is hard to believe for anything, be it healing, finances, or even your own salvation, beyond your knowledge of the Word of God. You may not get your healing if you do not know what the Word says about healing. You may not believe God for healing if you don't understand that He wants you well. If you are still thinking that God may want you sick for some reason, how can you go to Him in faith and receive healing?

Learn to know God's nature and what He has to say about sickness. God has always been opposed to sickness and disease. He has always made provision for His covenant people to get healed. If sickness was the will of God, He would not have called Himself by the name 'Jehovah Rapha'. His very name is healing. His very nature is love, goodness, and healing. He is the Lord that heals you.

> *"If you listen carefully to the voice of the LORD your God and do what is right in his eyes, if you pay attention to his commands and keep all his decrees, I will not bring on you any of the diseases I brought on the Egyptians, for I am the LORD, who heals you."*
> *(Exodus 15:26, NIV)*

God has never made anyone sick. Sickness never comes from God. Satan is the 'god of this world' and comes to kill, steal, and destroy. God declared that He is our healer. He came to give us life until it overflows.

> *"The thief's purpose is to steal and kill and destroy. My purpose is to give them a rich and satisfying life."*
> *(John 10:10, NLT)*

> *"You shall serve the LORD your God, and He will bless your bread and your water. And I will take sickness away from the midst of you. No one shall suffer miscarriage or be barren in your land; I will fulfill the number of your days."*
> *(Exodus 23:25-26, NKJV)*

I love that scripture because it says that we are to have no barrenness or miscarriages. We are to live a long, healthy life. I have used this scripture countless times to pray over women who are about to miscarry, and they delivered full-term babies. I have prayed for many women who could not conceive, and when I showed them in the Bible what was their inheritance, they conceived. God is faithful to watch over His Word to perform it.

> *"And the LORD said, 'That's right, and it means that I am watching, and I will certainly carry out all my plans.'"*
> *(Jeremiah 1:12, NLT)*

Some had received fertility treatments and still had not conceived, but the Word of God always works. One lady had been inseminated seven times and failed each time, but now she has a healthy little boy and is about to deliver twins. She had them by faith, believing that 'Hebrew' women (spiritual Hebrews) have the right to have babies.

Determine in your heart that God is a good God and that He came to bring us life.

> *"Christ has redeemed us from the curse of the law, being made a curse for us; for it is written, 'Cursed is everyone who hangs on a tree.'"*
> *(Galatians 3:13, NKJV)*

> *"When he calls on me, I will answer; I will be with him in trouble and rescue him and honor him. I will satisfy him with a full life and give him my salvation."*
> *(Psalm 91:15-16, TLB)*

God cannot satisfy you with a long life if you get sick and die before your time. The Word of God settles the issue of the willingness of God to heal.

PRAYER OF AFFIRMATION

Satan is the author of sickness and Jesus is the Healer. I choose Jesus and declare Jesus is my Healer. Since I accept Jesus as Healer, I speak to my body and say you will act healed. I am healed by the stripes on Jesus' back and I will not allow disease, sickness, or oppression to stay here. That is of the devil, and I say, "Get out", in Jesus' name.

What does God expect from us?

We read previously in Exodus 23 that as long as the children of Israel walked in obedience to the Word of God, they had no barrenness or miscarriages, and lived a long life. But when they walked in disobedience, their lives were a mess.

We must realize that we can't keep the laws of God either. When you are in disobedience, you doubt that you can receive healing. You will never receive anything from God on your own merits. But Jesus paid for our sins past, present, and future. We can receive our healing because of what Jesus did, not because of anything we are doing, have done, or failed to do.

You may even begin to think that this has nothing to do with you today, but you are wrong. God is the same today as He was in the Old Testament.

He made the same provision in the New Testament as He did in the Old Testament. *Jesus is the Provision.* Your job is to believe.

In the Old Testament, it was a type or shadow of Jesus that got them healed. Jesus was then and always will be the answer. I heard a pastor say that in the Old Testament Jesus was concealed and in the New Testament He is revealed.

I remember one day, when I was reading Proverbs 3 with its conditions before each promise, I began to cry—I realized that I had failed so many of the conditions.

"My son, forget not my law; but let thine heart keep my commandments (condition) for length of days, and long life, and peace, shall they add to thee (promise). Let not mercy and truth forsake thee: bind them about thy neck; write them

upon the table of thine heart (condition): So shalt thou find favour and good understanding in the sight of God and man (promise). Trust in the LORD *with all thine heart; and lean not unto thine own understanding. In all thy ways acknowledge him (condition), and he shall direct thy path (promise). Be not wise in thine own eyes: fear the* LORD, *and depart from evil (condition). It shall be health to thy navel, and marrow to thy bones (promise)."*
(Proverbs 3:1-8, **promise/condition entries are mine***)*

All the way down through the passage as I read I found that I had failed to keep the conditions. Sometimes I didn't trust the Lord with all my heart. I always tried but kept failing. Through tears and feeling like a failure I asked the Lord, 'How is this going to work for me?'

Then I got to verse 25:

"Be not afraid of sudden fear, neither of the desolation of the wicked, when it cometh."
(Proverbs 3:25)

I began to shout when I got to verse 26:

"For the LORD *shall be thy confidence, and shall keep thy foot from being taken."*
(Proverbs 3:26)

God keeps me safe! Hallelujah! I realized that God knew I couldn't keep the law (the covenant) so the Father sent Jesus to keep it for me. Did Jesus fail in His mission to make provision for me? NO! NO! A thousand times NO! What Jesus did is so much more powerful than Adam's failure.

"Blessed be the God and the Father of our Lord Jesus Christ,

which according to his abundant mercy hath begotten us
again unto a lively hope by the resurrection of Jesus Christ
from the dead, to an inheritance incorruptible, and
undefiled, and that fadeth not away, reserved in heaven for
you, who are kept by the power of God through faith unto
salvation ready to be revealed in the last time."
(1 Peter 1:3-5)

We need to remember that our sin is none of the devil's business. Jesus took care of our sin. Satan has no right to bring it up in condemnation (Romans 8:1). Glory to God! This is how I will make it. I will look to the Lamb who became that snake on the pole for me so that I could be healed (Numbers 21:8). Why was it a snake and not a lamb? Because Jesus became sin for me; He took my place.

"For God made Christ, who never sinned, to be the offering for
our sin, so that we could be made right with God through Christ."
(2 Corinthians 5:21, NLT)

"And the LORD *will take away from thee all sickness, and will*
put none of the evil diseases of Egypt, which thou knowest,
upon thee; but will lay them upon all them that hate thee."
(Deuteronomy 7:15)

That promise is for us today!

"If ye be Christ's, then are ye Abraham's seed, and heirs according
to the promise."
(Galatians 3:29)

This tells me that I am the seed of Abraham and, as such, I have a right to claim the promises. So don't ever let anyone tell you that there is something wrong with you and that is why you can't get healed. There is nothing wrong with God, there is nothing wrong with Jesus, there is nothing wrong with the Word, and there is nothing wrong with you.

There is nothing wrong with you because Jesus made you a new creation. Old things passed away and all things have become new. You still have the same body, but it was your spirit that was made new. Jesus now lives in your spirit. When God examines you, He deals only with Jesus. Jesus is your sacrifice and He is perfect. Dear one, see now that there is nothing wrong with you because Jesus lives in you and that makes you okay. You have to meditate on who God says you are to be able to grasp this truth.

If you will enforce what the Word says about you and not base what you believe on anything other than what God said in His Word, the symptoms in your body and the tests of the doctors will eventually have to line up and show that what the Word said is absolutely true.

He told us that by His stripes we are healed, and He didn't ask your opinion as to whether you are healed or not. If God says I am healed by the stripes of Jesus, who am I to argue with Him? Who are the symptoms, the pain, the doctor's report, or my body to argue with the Mighty One of Israel? I enforce only what He told me in His Word.

Who does God say He is?
Remember, God said He is the Healer, Jehovah Rapha. Why would God call Himself 'Healer' if He were opposed to healing? We are to mimic Jesus and He was never sick. I am sure He was tempted to be sick because the Word says He was tempted in all points like we are.

> *"For we have not an high priest which cannot be touched with the feeling of our infirmities; but was in all points tempted like as we are, yet without sin."*
> *(Hebrews 4:15)*

Jesus is our example of what God is like. Jesus was never sick except when He took our sicknesses on the cross. Sickness is a part of the curse.

> *"The* LORD *will afflict you with the boils of Egypt and with tumors, scurvy, and the itch, from which you cannot be cured. The* LORD *will strike you with madness, blindness, and panic. You will grope around in broad daylight like a blind person groping in the darkness, but you will not find your way. You will be oppressed and robbed continually, and no one will come to save you."*
> *(Deuteronomy 28:27-29, NLT)*

> *"These plagues will be intense and without relief, making you miserable and unbearably sick. He will afflict you with all the diseases of Egypt that you feared so much, and you will have no relief. The* LORD *will afflict you with every sickness and plague there is, even those not mentioned in this Book of Instruction, until you are destroyed."*
> *(Deuteronomy 28:59-61, NLT)*

The curses described above were the penalty for being disobedient to the law. We can be thankful for the following scripture in Galatians 3:13.

> *"But Christ has rescued us from the curse pronounced by the law. When he was hung on the cross, he took upon himself the curse for our wrongdoing. For it is written in the Scriptures, 'Cursed is everyone who is hung on a tree.'"*
> *(Galatians 3:13, NLT)*

We can praise the Lord for what Jesus did in taking our place and paying the penalty for our sin. The curse could not stick to Jesus' body, and we should confess that sickness cannot stick to our bodies either. As Jesus is, so are we in this world (1 John 4:17).

Religion may have a problem with changing natural circumstances with mere confession of the Word of God, but God spoke and the worlds were framed. God's words have power in them. Our words have power in them. We can change our world by speaking to it.

> *"The tongue can bring death or life; those who love to talk will reap the consequences."*
> *(Proverbs 18:21, NLT)*

PRAYER OF AFFIRMATION

This body is the temple of the Holy Spirit. Sickness and disease cannot stick to me. I walk in health just like Jesus did. I declare that every disease, every germ, and all sickness have to die when they touch my body. Viruses and infections cannot live in me. Cancer, diabetes, or any other disease must leave me now! I put up an eviction notice and say, "Get out!" I will not house the curse.

Healing was Done at Calvary

> *"Yet it was our weaknesses he carried; it was our sorrows that weighed him down. And we thought his troubles were a punishment from God, a punishment for his own sins! But he was pierced for our rebellion, crushed for our sins. He was beaten so we could be whole. He was whipped so we could be healed."*
> *(Isaiah 53:4-5, NLT)*

> *"He personally carried our sins in his body on the cross so that we can be dead to sin and live for what is right. By his wounds you are healed."*
> *(1 Peter 2:24, NLT)*

Decide that you know that the deed has been done. Jesus finished His work at Calvary to pay not only for our sins but also for our healing. He does not have to come back and do anything else. He could have gone to Calvary, been nailed to the cross, died, and risen again just so that we would be saved, and only saved, by believing in what He had done. But, praise God, He didn't stop there! He took those awful stripes on His back—He took thirty-nine of them— so that you and I could be free of sickness and disease.

He left absolutely nothing undone! The wounds on His brow were for our peace of mind. The wounds in His hands were to bless the work of our hands. The wounds in His feet were to bless our walk of faith, and represent our dominion on the earth that He purchased for us with His blood. The wound in His side was so that you and I could be accepted in the Beloved. The stripes on His back were for the healing of our bodies.

Thorns in Bible times always represented the curse. When they placed that crown made of thorns on His precious brow, and the blood began to flow, we were redeemed from the curse.

Jesus did not fail. His work on the cross was complete. In fact, it was so complete that miracles continue to happen every day just so that we can be free.

People pray that Jesus will heal them, when actually He already has. The only thing left for you to do is to receive what He did on the cross and lay hold of the healing that was paid for you some two thousand years ago.

"O LORD, if you heal me, I will be truly healed; if you save me, I will be truly saved. My praises are for you alone!" (Jeremiah 17:14, NLT)

Aren't you thrilled that God not only is willing to heal you, but to also forgive you? It is the express will of God to provide healing *and* forgiveness. Read these scriptures out loud and shout for joy!

"And when they could not come nigh unto him for the press, they uncovered the roof where he was: and when they had

broken it up, they let down the bed wherein the sick of the palsy lay. When Jesus saw their faith, he said unto the sick of the palsy, Son, thy sins be forgiven thee. But there was certain of the scribes sitting there, and reasoning in their hearts, Why doth this man thus speak blasphemies? who can forgive sins but God only? And immediately when Jesus perceived in his spirit that they so reasoned within themselves, he said unto them, Why reason ye these things in your hearts? Whether is it easier to say to the sick of the palsy, Thy sins be forgiven thee; or to say, Arise, and take up thy bed, and walk?"
(Mark 2:4-9)

"Bless the LORD, *O my soul: and all that is within me, bless his holy name. Bless the* LORD, *O my soul, and forget not all his benefits: who forgiveth all thine iniquites; who healeth all they diseases; who redeemeth thy life from destruction; who crowneth thee with lovingkindness and tender mercies; who satisfieth thy mouth with good things; so that thy youth is renewed like the eagles."*
(Psalm 103:1-5)

"Beloved, I pray that you may prosper in every way and [that your body] may keep well, even as [I know] your soul keeps well and prospers."
(3 John 1:2, AMP)

A lady who had been in a wheelchair for several years told me she was believing for healing and kept saying, 'Someday Jesus is going to heal me and I will get up out of this wheelchair.' One day the Spirit of God spoke to her and said, 'I am not going to heal you some day. I healed you when I took the stripes on My back. You will get out of that chair when you believe it.' She got up and walked, and is still walking today.

If you tell me that *someday* Jesus is going to heal you, I know that you are probably going to remain sick. I have had people tell me that, and I have attended their funeral. FAITH IS NOW! Don't keep putting healing off until 'some day'. *Receive it now by faith*. He did His job perfectly, now He expects us to do our job. Our job is to lay hold of what belongs to us.

PRAYER OF AFFIRMATION

I thank You, Father, that Your Word is true. I choose now to believe that You have healed me at Calvary and I receive that healing now. I see my sickness on Your back that was striped for me. I have been redeemed from the curse of the law and I lay hold of my healing. I come out of agreement with any lies that I may have believed concerning Your Word. I covenant with you to put Your Word first place in my life, in the name of Jesus.

CHAPTER 2 NOTES AND REFLECTIONS

Chapter 3

HOW TO RECEIVE YOUR HEALING

What is Faith?

Remember that anything you get from God you will get by faith. You will get it either by your own faith, or someone else's faith. Faith is how you got saved and faith is one way you can get healed.

Faith is simply believing what you have been promised but cannot see with your physical eyes at the present time. Faith is confidence in God and His Word.

> *"Now faith is the assurance (the confirmation, the title deed) of the things [we] hope for, being the proof of things [we] do not see and the conviction of their reality [faith perceiving as real fact what is not revealed to the senses]."*
> *(Hebrews 11:1, AMP)*

> *"You can never please God without faith, without depending on him. Anyone who wants to come to God must believe that there is a God and that he rewards those who sincerely look for him."*
> *(Hebrews 11:6, TLB)*

Unbelief will stop the flow of God's power. Even Jesus could do no mighty miracles in his own hometown because of their unbelief.

"And he did not many mighty works there because of their unbelief."
(Matthew 13:58)

What you receive from God you must receive by faith. God does not meet your needs or heal your body because of His love for you. God's love for you is what sent Jesus to the cross to purchase your healing.

No matter how drastic the need, it is not need that will get you healed. Faith is what will get your needs met and your body healed—faith in the finished work of Jesus on the cross. Your lack of belief can hinder your receiving.

If anything other than faith moved God, the enemy would have God running all over the place. Needs are not what causes God to act on your behalf. We know that God loves everyone, so He is not compelled to heal you because of His great love for you. Only faith in the obedience of Jesus to go to the cross will cause you to receive your healing.

The only way to receive faith is to get into His Word. The Bible says:

"Faith comes by hearing, and hearing by the Word of God."
(Romans 10:17, NKJV)

"For whatever is born of God is victorious over the world;
and this is the victory that conquers the world, even our faith.
Who is it that is victorious over [that conquers] the world but
he who believes that Jesus is the Son of God [who adheres to,
trusts in, and relies on that fact]?"
(1 John 5:4-5, AMP)

"My son, attend to my words; consent and submit to my

sayings. Let them not depart from your sight; keep them in the center of your heart. For they are life to those who find them, healing and health to all their flesh. Keep and guard your heart with all vigilance and above all that you guard, for out of it flow the springs of life."
(Proverbs 4:20-23, AMP)

"My child, pay attention to what I say. Listen carefully to my words. Don't lose sight of them. Let them penetrate deep into your heart, for they bring life to those who find them, and healing to their whole body. Guard your heart above all else, for it determines the course of your life."
(Proverbs 4:20-23, NLT)

"But without faith it is impossible to please him: for he that cometh to God must believe that he is, and that he is a rewarder of them that diligently seek him."
(Hebrews 11:6)

Do you see that faith is how we receive eternal life, and without faith you cannot please God? We need to live by faith.

"And the LORD answered me, and said, Write the vision, and make it plain upon tables, that he may run that readeth it. For the vision is yet for an appointed time, but at the end it shall speak, and not lie: though it tarry, wait for it; because it will surely come, it will not tarry. Behold, his soul which is lifted up is not upright in him: but the just shall live by his faith."
(Habakkuk 2:2-4)

Where is our Faith, and What is the Purpose of It?

Faith does not come out of your head, but rather faith is an 'inner man' issue. Faith comes out of your heart. Faith connects you to the unlimited power of God. Faith will give you God's ability.

If I find out what God can do, I can figure out what faith can do. Is anything too hard for God? No. With God nothing is impossible. With God all things are possible.

"There is nothing too hard for thee:"
(Jeremiah 32:17b)

Faith can say to a mountain, 'Move and be cast into the sea,' and the mountain will obey faith. Do you see that we are commanded to live by our faith? Your faith comes by hearing the Word of God. We received the measure of His faith and now we live by His faith, and that means a steady diet of the Word of God.

Now, if we are going to get to a place where faith will work for us like it did for Jesus, we will have to grow in faith. That may be your issue. Jesus had faith and it was highly developed when He walked this earth. Jesus could get His faith to work very quickly. He was our example and He told us to do the things He did.

Remember Matthew 17, when Jesus told Peter to go fishing because they needed tax money? Jesus listened to His Father and obeyed Him by telling Peter to go catch a fish and the tax money would be there.

Jesus did all He did by faith. He even went to the cross by faith. He had never seen God put all the sins of the world on anyone, then watch that person go to hell, pay the price for sin, and then get the person out of hell. Do you see that He died in faith expecting the Father to raise Him out of the depths of hell?

We can totally trust our Father just like our example, Jesus, did.

What Actually Belongs to Us?

Doesn't the Word of God say that we are joint heirs with Christ? Everything that belongs to Jesus belongs to us? He purchased it for us. That does not mean I get half and He gets the other half. When you are joint heirs, it all belongs to Him and it all belongs to us. If you have joint custody, that means you have equal custody.

"That the Gentiles should be fellow heirs, and of the same body, and partakers of his promise in Christ by the gospel."
(Ephesians 3:6)

"And if children, then heirs; heirs of God, and joint-heirs with Christ; if so be that we suffer with him, that we may be also glorified together."
(Romans 8:17)

How Do We Build Our Faith?

You build your faith by feeding on the Word of God. Feed that habit. Get hooked on the Word. Try to overdose on the Word of God. Take it day and night. Listen to what God told Joshua:

"This book of the law shall not depart out of thy mouth; but thou shalt meditate therein day and night, that thou mayest observe to do according to all that is written therein: for then thou shalt make thy way prosperous, and then thou shalt have good success."
(Joshua 1:8)

Not all success is good. There are plenty of men who have 'world-defined' success. They have a huge bank account, houses, cars, and material possessions, and yet they are dying with cancer or some other terminal disease. That, my friend, is not good success. If you want to have good success, which is healing, prosperity, peace in your heart, and freedom from guilt and shame, do what the Word told Joshua to do in the scripture above.

We read in Proverbs 4 that the Word is medicine to your flesh. It will feed you and then make you hungry for more. Use the Word of God to make you strong in your faith. We have underestimated the power of faith. Our faith has the same power that Jesus' faith had. The Word has strength in it. If you want to be strong in your spirit, make a daily habit of spending time in the Word.

"But if the Spirit of him that raised up Jesus from the dead dwell in you, he that raised up Christ from the dead shall also quicken your mortal bodies by his Spirit that dwelleth in you."
(Romans 8:11)

I realize I am pushing the Word of God in a big way, but it is the only way I know that will allow you to live the life Jesus promised.

Words of Faith

"The prophet who has a dream, let him tell his dream; but he who has My word, let him speak My Word faithfully. What has straw in common with wheat [for nourishment]? says the Lord. Is not My word like fire [that consumes all that cannot endure the test]? says the Lord, and like a hammer that breaks in pieces the rock [of most stubborn resistance]?"
(Jeremiah 23:28-29, AMP)

'But he who has My word, let him speak My word faithfully'—do you see it?

According to this scripture we can take the Word of God and hammer the mountain in our life—it will move if you apply enough pressure to it. God was not talking about real estate or geography when He told us to speak to the mountain. The mountain represents the problems, sickness, or circumstances and storms in our lives.

He told us to speak *to* the mountain, not to speak *about* the mountain. What have you been saying *to* your mountain? Are you trying to make peace with it, or agreeing with it? Or are you commanding it by the Word to be removed? Are you 'hammering' on it with the Word? Only the Word is like a hammer. If you don't talk to that mountain it will surely talk to you, especially during the night. It will tell you that you are going to die. It will tell you that bad things are going to happen to you and your family. Speak out loud to those voices and tell them what the Word says about you and your circumstances.

> *"Truly I tell you, whoever says to this mountain, Be lifted up and thrown into the sea! and does not doubt at all in his heart but believes that what he says will take place, it will be done for him. For this reason I am telling you, whatever you ask for in prayer, believe (trust and be confident) that it is granted to you, and you will [get it]."*
> *(Mark 11:23-24, AMP)*

> *"For verily I say unto you, That whosoever shall say unto this mountain, Be thou removed, and be thou cast into the sea; and shall not doubt in his heart, but shall believe that those things which he saith shall come to pass; he shall have whatsoever he saith. Therefore I say unto you, What things so ever ye desire, when ye pray, believe that ye receive them, and ye shall have them."*
> *(Mark 11:23-24)*

Believe that you have received!

PRAYER OF AFFIRMATION

My body is quickened and made alive by the same power that raised Jesus from the dead. Herein is our love made perfect, that we may have boldness in the day of judgment: because as He is, so are we in this world. He is not sick and neither am I. He is not depressed, and neither am I. I confess that as He is so am I in this world. I am crucified with Christ, nevertheless I live, yet not I but Christ who lives in me, if Christ lives in me, He is not sick and neither am I. I charge this body, 'Get in line with what the Word says about me.'

CHAPTER 3 NOTES AND REFLECTIONS

Chapter 4

ADMINISTERING HEALING

Ways to Administer and Receive Healing

"He said to them, 'Go into all the world and preach the gospel to all creation. Whoever believes and is baptized will be saved, but whoever does not believe will be condemned. And these signs will accompany those who believe: In my name they will drive out demons; they will speak in new tongues; they will pick up snakes with their hands; and when they drink deadly poison, it will not hurt them at all; they will place their hands on sick people, and they will get well.'" (Mark 16:15-18, NIV)

The Bible promises that these signs will follow the believer. We can receive our healing based on these promises.

There are several ways for the believer to receive healing:
- Laying on of hands.
- Prayer of agreement.
- Calling on the elders and anointing with oil.
- Receiving Communion.

Your body is the temple of the Holy Spirit and you should get enough rest, stay out from under stress as much as possible, eat right (no junk food), and drink plenty of water.

Even if you have violated those laws you can still be healed. God is a merciful God and no matter how badly you have missed it, Jesus did not miss it and you can receive your healing just because He loves you. He will meet you where your faith is.

Laying on of Hands

Before laying hands on people for healing, I suggest that you spend some time being intimate with the Lord, if at all possible. When you spend time with Him, worshipping Him, praising Him, and finding out what it is He wants to impart to you, you will go away from Him with His fragrance on you. Ask God for wisdom to know what to do; He has an answer for every question, every problem or situation.

> *"If you need wisdom, ask our generous God, and he will give*
> *it to you. He will not rebuke you for asking."*
> *(James 1:5, NLT)*

Sometimes when I hug my husband I will pick up the scent of his cologne on my clothes, then when I hug someone else they will pick up the same fragrance. That is how it is with God. Spend time with Him and you will find you smell like Him when you lay your hands on someone else.

Any born-again Christian can lay their hands on a person so that they can receive healing. Nevertheless, you should prepare for an appointment with God so that you will be more equipped to be used by God. It is an appointment where you meet with God and allow Him to use your hands to be a conduit for the Holy Spirit to flow through you to that person needing healing.

We can learn to use our faith as a tool. Just like you would take a hammer and nail to hang a picture on the wall, you can take your faith and put your hand on the person needing healing. You should realize you are not the healer, but that you are being obedient to do what we are told in Mark 16: 'And they will place their hands on the sick people and they will get well.' God will meet you there.

You do not have to push or be loud. Sometimes you may be loud, but remember God is not deaf and He is not nervous! Be aware of those around you, as well as the person you are ministering to. You should be gentle and allow God to speak to you as you are praying. Always pray the Scriptures. **Never pray:** 'Father, if it be Thy will, heal this person.' That is not scriptural. He has already told us it is His will for them to be healed.

Learn to listen as you pray. Not only to the person for whom you are praying, but listen to God. Before you begin ask them what it is they want from God and then start to pray about their request. Believe that God has placed you here and that you are an instrument in His hands. Believe in the gift that is in you.

Expect God to move through you and never be moved by what you see. I have gone to the hospital to pray for people who looked more dead than alive. I have learned to look at what I am believing for, not what my eyes see.

I recently spoke with a lady in church who came to thank me for coming to the hospital to pray for her. When I went to pray for her she was in a coma, and there were not many signs of life in her. I did not look at what I saw before my eyes, I looked at what faith said. She was in the hospital for over eighty days, but she is alive and well today. Praise the Lord!

I also remember going to pray for a lady who had been in a coma for three days before being discovered lying on the floor. Her blood sugar was over 900. The nurses said she was dying, but a friend and I went in and began to declare what the Word said about her. We bound the spirit of death and began to call her spirit strong and alive. We told the devil it was going to be as we said, because we were saying what the Word said. Death was strong in that room, but Jesus touched her body and the next morning when we went back to check on her, she was sitting up in a chair eating.

She has since joined the church and is doing well. I see her in church often.

When you are praying for someone, God may say to you, 'Tell them they should drink more water,' or 'Tell them to forgive their mother.' He will show you the source of the problem.

Do not go off on a tangent praying about something else that God may or may not have shown you. Pray about what they asked for; then, if God shows you something else, you can share it as long as you are sure that it came from God.

There are things that God has shown me about people that He never intended me to share. He will show you things to enable you to know more accurately how to pray. He will never show you anything so that you can embarrass the person or show people how used of God you are. There are things I know by the Spirit that I probably will never share. Be wise in dealing with precious people. God has entrusted you with a tremendous responsibility. Do not take it lightly.

Remember, we are not here to impress anyone with how well we can pray. We are not here to build a name for ourselves. We are here to show the love of God to anyone who is sick and has come forward for healing.

Also remember, people are not coming to the altar for your advice. They are there to be healed. This is not a counseling session. There may be times when God gives you a word for someone, but be careful you don't give 'unasked for' advice. You may have an opportunity to help them in that area later, but remember why you are there, **and why they are there.**

For example, suppose they tell you that their husband beat them up. Don't pray for their neighbors to hear the ruckus and intervene, and do not tell them to leave their husband, or that they should file for divorce. Even if you feel like that, keep it to yourself. Wait for them to tell you what they want from God.

If they tell you that they are having trouble with pornography, do not pray loudly, 'Lord, help this person stay away from pornography.'

Use the intelligence God gave you to pray with discretion. Treat the person like you would like to be treated. Do not embarrass them.

Do not tell people anything that cannot be backed up by scripture. For example, 'God just told me that He is not going to heal you today.' That is not scriptural. Remember, He only speaks the Word.

There will be many times when there is an instant manifestation of healing, but many times we lay hands on people in faith just expecting. So do not be disappointed or show sadness if there is no outward manifestation. When I lay my hands on a person, I expect that God has done the work. If I see nothing, it does not matter. I put my faith out there and don't take it back until the healing manifests, no matter how long it takes.

Many times I will hear later that healing came when they got home or within a few days. I believe that healing always comes. It may not always be received, but I believe when I ask in Jesus' name according to His will, He always answers my prayers.

Jesus said, 'You shall lay hands on the sick and they shall recover' (Mark 16:18). Sometimes recovery takes a while. Don't be impatient. Leave the timing to God.

Prayer of Agreement

"Again I say unto you, That if two of you shall agree on earth as touching any thing that they shall ask, it shall be done for them of my Father which is in heaven."
Matthew 18:19)

We should agree with the person for their healing. You should tell the person to stand for their healing. It does not matter if they feel or see anything. Healing comes, and if we receive it as truth over the outward facts, the symptoms *will* go.

The enemy is good at what he does. He will try and discourage you with pain, swelling, outward symptoms, even tests and the doctor's report. But just remember what the Word says:

"What do ye imagine against the LORD? he will make an utter end: affliction shall not rise up the second time." (Nahum 1:9)

Satan does not have the legal right to put a disease back on you after you received your healing. Stand your ground. Tell that disease what the Word says.

Don't argue with anyone that asks for prayer. I have had people come up for prayer and they then try to argue with me about whether it is God's will to be healed or not. I even had a lady ask me to lay hands on her for healing and she told me that she didn't believe that God healed anymore, and in fact didn't believe God existed! I really wanted to ask her why she even bothered to come up for prayer and tell her that she might as well go sit down. But, in spite of what I was thinking, I chose to be kind to her—she was there, so God must have drawn her there. Actually, she still shows up every now and then.

Sometimes I have seen God do a miracle just to show people His power in action because He loves them. Generally, though, He requires faith. God doesn't perform tricks; He operates by faith with miracles following. Always be kind and gentle in your actions and speech, and always leave the results to God. He knows what He is doing and He is in charge of the situation at hand.

Don't be shocked at the things people say. We have had people swear, say bad things, and use terrible language in front of us. Remember, God will heal anyone that believes He heals. Sometimes the people who come for healing have not accepted Him as their Savior. God will use the healing they desire to prove His love for them. Be patient with people. Remember, they are precious to God.

Probably the first recorded healing in the Old Testament is when God healed Abimelech's household. Abimelech was a Gentile, a heathen king, but the mercy of God was there and he and his household were healed.

"So Abraham prayed unto God: and God healed Abimelech, and his wife, and his maidservants; and they bare children."
(Genesis 20:17)

God loves people and we must do the same. Healing is God's dinner bell, and sometimes He heals people who are not saved, but have faith for healing. He will heal them and they may accept Him as Savior later. I prayed for a non-believing lady once who was in a coma dying of liver disease and almost instantly God healed her. When I talked to her at home after she was healed, I could not get her to pray the sinner's prayer with me. I planted seeds and she knows it was God that healed her. That was forty years ago and as far as I know she is still alive. I believe she will be saved before she leaves this earth!

Anointing with Oil

Again, this is not about you. This is not your show. This is all about Him and His glory. There is a place to anoint with oil. Listen to the Lord and do what He tells you.

On a side note, I personally do not usually anoint unbelievers with oil. This is my personal belief; I am not suggesting that this is doctrine. I believe that James was talking to the church when he asked if there was any sick among them (James 5:14). As a result of my belief, I lay hands on unbelievers and believe God for healing, but I don't anoint them with oil. I anoint believers with oil. If I can get a person to believe God for healing even when they have not received Him as their Savior, God will meet them where their faith is and will use that to show them His goodness. Many times they accept Him as Savior as well as Healer.

"Is any sick among you? let him call for the elders of the church; and let them pray over him, anointing him with oil in the name of the Lord: And the prayer of faith shall save the sick, and the Lord shall raise him up; and if he have committed

sins, they shall be forgiven him. Confess your faults one to another, and pray one for another, that ye may be healed. The effectual fervent prayer of a righteous man availeth much." (James 5:14-16)

One thing that might be helpful to you as you minister to those that are unconscious is to remember that their spirit is alive. It does not go into a coma, it does not sleep, and it does not die. I have prayed for a few people who were in a coma and just said a simple prayer of salvation, and they have come out of the coma a different person. Their spirit can hear you.

I went to the hospital to pray for a man in his sixties who was in a coma. They had taken his leg off and, according to the doctors, he was dying. His sister asked me to go to the hospital and pray for him because the doctor said he was not going to make it, and he was not born again. I went in and talked to his spirit. I told him I was going to pray a prayer to accept Jesus and if he believed that Jesus is the Son of God and would like to accept him, all he had to do was agree. I prayed the sinner's prayer, and then I laid my hand on his head and asked the Lord to allow healing to come and to let him leave a testimony. Three months later he showed up at the altar and asked me if I was Pastor Evelyn. I said, 'Yes,' and he said, 'You are the one that came and led me to Jesus, and I want you to know I got saved.' He danced around up there and praised the Lord. He and his grandchildren are at church every Sunday. He is leaving a testimony everywhere he goes.

Receiving Communion

You can receive your healing through the partaking of Holy Communion. You do not have to be in a church building or meeting to take Communion. You can get some bread or a cracker, some grape juice, and pray over it and give yourself Communion.

As you partake of Holy Communion, begin seeing and declaring how you have been healed by Jesus' stripes, and how His blood has washed away all your sins and qualified you to receive His healing and health.

Holy Communion Prayer

Hold the bread in your hand and say:

Thank You, Jesus, for Your broken body. Thank You for bearing my symptoms and sicknesses at the cross so that I may have Your health and wholeness. I declare that by Your stripes, by the beatings You bore, by the lashes which fell on Your back, I am completely healed. I believe and I receive Your resurrection life in my body today.

(Eat the bread)

(I always say and you may want to add) *I look back to the cross and forward to Your coming, and thank You for what You did and are doing.*

Next take the cup in your hand and say:

Thank You, Jesus, for Your blood that has washed me whiter than snow. Your blood has brought me forgiveness and made me righteous forever. And, as I drink, I celebrate and partake of the inheritance of the righteous, which includes preservation, healing, wholeness, and all Your blessings.

(Drink the wine/juice)

What about the anointing?

Guard the anointing that God has placed on your life. You would not desire to pray for the sick unless God put the desire there. So guard the anointing like the treasure that it is.

There may be things that God will ask you *not* to do that seem to be ok for others to do. Don't question why you can't do them. If God puts a 'check' in your spirit about something, stop right there!

You need to be a clean vessel for God to flow through. Remember, 'it is not about you!' We lay our lives down for Christ's sake.

"And it shall come to pass in that day, that his burden shall be taken away from off thy shoulder, and his yoke from off thy neck, and the yoke shall be destroyed because of the anointing."
(Isaiah 10:27)

The anointing is the yoke-destroying, burden-removing power of God. You have that same anointing within you that Jesus had, and it is there to help you as you lay your hands on people. I have noticed that the stronger the anointing, the more powerful the results.

"But the anointing which ye have received of him abideth in you, and ye need not that any man teach you: but as the same anointing teacheth you of all things, and is truth, and is no lie, and even as it hath taught you, ye shall abide in him."
(1 John 2:27)

Check Your Strife

"For where envying and strife is, there is confusion and every evil work."
(James 3:16)

Keep your life free from strife. James tells us in this verse that 'with strife comes every evil work'. Keep that door shut or someone else will have to lay hands on you to set you free. You may be thinking, 'This is too hard. I didn't know I had to do all this.' The Bible says, 'The way of transgressors is hard' (Proverbs 13:15). It is a wonderful pleasure to be used by God to help others. Remember God's 'thing' is people. What an honor for us as His children that He would let us minister to those who mean so much to Him.

Remember this: you do not have to be perfect to minister to people. If that were so, God would have no one He could use. You just need to have a heart for people and a deep love for God. You need a heart willing to learn all you can in order to be God's healing hand extended.

Keep in mind what an honor it is that God would put such confidence in you and would allow you to lay your hands on His precious children.

Some Practical Reminders as You Pray for Others

- Be sure you have a breath mint (check your breath).
- Be sure you are clean and represent the Lord well in your appearance.
- Ladies, be sure you are dressed appropriately (no exposed parts).
- Be careful not to touch people inappropriately; lay hands on either their heads or their shoulders.
- It is always good to have men pray for men and ladies pray for ladies.
- Always, always remember we are here to show the love of God.
- Keep a thankful heart and a good attitude.
- Be very careful not to show unusual facial expressions over those you are praying for; don't sigh or roll your eyes even as they walk away. Remember that body language speaks loudly— they may not see you do it, but someone else may.

CHAPTER 4 NOTES AND REFLECTIONS

_____

_____

_____

_____

_____

_____

_____

_____

_____

_____

_____

_____

_____

_____

_____

_____

_____

_____

Chapter 5

CONDEMNATION AND OTHER LIES

Condemnation Has No Place in My Life

"So now there is no condemnation for those who belong to Christ Jesus."
(Romans 8:1, NLT)

I am convinced that condemnation is one of the biggest reasons why people don't receive their healing. They think, 'I didn't get healed because of what I have done, or by what I have not done.'

Healing is a gift, and it was paid for in full by the stripes on Jesus' back. All we have to do is receive it by faith.

A friend of mine and I went to the hospital to pray for a man with a cancerous tumor in his throat. He was in ICU, hooked up to a machine with a tube in his throat. The doctors had given him a terrible report. Now this man had smoked for years and abused his body, and I could see that he didn't think he was worthy of healing.

I simply leaned over him and asked him, 'Could you just get healed, not because of anything you have done or not done, but just because Jesus paid for it?' A big tear trickled down his face as he nodded his head yes. He was totally healed, not with medicine or surgery. God touched his body and he was totally healed within six weeks. I am sure he did not live a perfect life. He was not healed based on his own merit. He was healed because of the mercy and love of God. Remember, God's grace is sufficient.

Now I ask you the same question, 'Could you just get healed, simply because Jesus paid for it? Not because of anything you have done or failed to do. Could you just receive your healing?' You cannot do enough to earn your healing through works. You cannot perform enough good deeds, read enough chapters in your Bible, pray long enough and hard enough, or even torture yourself enough to pay for your healing. You cannot even fast long enough to deserve your healing. Just receive the healing that Jesus purchased for you.

If it were left up to us to achieve healing, we would be in sad shape. It is Jesus plus NOTHING!

The enemy will try and tell you that there must be something wrong with you and that is why you cannot receive your healing. As I have told you before, there is nothing wrong with you because the old man died and the new man is perfect. God never told me I had to be perfect to come for healing. He told me to come to Him in faith. He said, 'The old man has passed away.' I was born again into the image of God. In order to come out from under condemnation you will need to find out who you are in Christ.

"Therefore as by the offence of one judgment came upon all men to condemnation; even so by the righteousness of one the free gift came upon all men unto justification of life."
(Romans 5:18)

You were not a sinner because you have sinned, you were a sinner because Adam sinned.

"For as by one man's disobedience many were made sinners, so by the obedience of one shall many be made righteous."
(Romans 5:19)

You are not righteous because of anything you have done, you are righteous because of what Jesus did.

"For he hath made him to be sin for us, who knew no sin; that we might be made the righteousness of God in him."
(2 Corinthians 5:21)

All that is necessary for you to do to obtain healing is to receive what was already done. The newest believer is as righteous as the oldest saint.

"For if by one man's offence death reigned by one; much more they which receive abundance of grace and of the gift of righteousness shall reign in life by one, Jesus Christ."
(Romans 5:17)

Righteousness is a gift and it comes by accepting Jesus as your Savior. When you make Jesus your Savior, you are a righteous believer and have a covenant with Jehovah God. Realizing this, you can pursue what He has promised in His Word.

About eight years ago I was studying about righteousness and was excited about my right standing with God. I had a mammogram at around that time. The technician called me and said I should come back. I went to the clinic the next week. They told me I should go to the Cancer Center. When I arrived the nurse met me and told me that we had to find out what we were going to do about this. I asked, 'What are we going to do about what?' She replied, 'About this large mass in your right breast.' I told her I didn't have a mass in my breast. I told her, 'I am the righteousness of God in Christ and as such, tumors, cancers, growths, and masses can't live in me.'

She said, 'Yes, you do have a mass, and you don't understand—this is what we are looking for when we do these tests. We have a doctor on site who will tell us how radical this has to be.' I thought to myself, 'I can tell you how radical it will be, you are not taking my parts!' But I said, 'You don't understand, I am the righteousness of God in Christ and this can't live in me.'

I'm sure she thought I had lost my mind or that I was in shock or something, but I began to tell her about Jesus and how she could make Him her Savior. When she was finished doing the tests, she said to me. 'Sit here and don't worry. I will be gone about an hour and will return with the doctor to talk with you.' I told her that I had learned years ago not to worry. I said to her, 'I put the blood of Jesus on those pictures and on my breast. You go look at the x-rays, for all is well.'

At that moment I didn't care what she thought. I was fighting for my body and I knew what I was supposed to have. I kept my conversation right and didn't let my heart get troubled. It didn't seem like much time had passed before she returned. She told me that they couldn't explain it, but they had one picture with a large mass and another one that was clear. She said, 'You are the best patient I have ever had!' I am sure that is true because I wasn't full of fear. Build your 'faith house' before the storm hits and you will be able to stand when the trouble comes.

I trust this will help you to understand that when you know what belongs to you, and you have taken the time to get that down into your spirit, you can go after what belongs to you and receive it. Stop fear at the door with what the Word of God says.

Never Look at the Circumstances!

Once hands are laid on you, never look at the circumstances. Pay no attention to lying symptoms.

> *"Those who hold on to worthless idols abandon their loyalty to you."*
> (Jonah 2:8, GW)

> *"They that wait upon lying vanities forsake their own mercy."*
> (Jonah 2:8, 1599 Geneva Bible)

The biblical meaning of 'vanities' is 'emptiness or nothingness, trouble or wickedness, vapor'. Do you see that anything can become an idol to you, even your sickness? That sickness begins to consume you. Take cancer, for instance—it consumes you and your whole family. It is all you think about. It takes all your time, your thought life, your finances, and your energy. It begins to take over. It is an enemy of God. You are not an enemy of God, but the thing that you are consumed with and is trying to kill your body is an enemy of God.

You cannot look at symptoms, the pain, the report, or listen to what others are saying. You must look at what God's Word says about the thing that is trying to take you out of this world. God never told us to stand for a while and then turn and run. He said having done all to stand, stand therefore (Ephesians 6:13). No matter the pain, no matter the doctor's report, no matter the results of the MRI, CT scan or x-rays, stand firm on the Word and what it says.

Tests and doctors have been known to be wrong. God's Word is never wrong, has never been known to be wrong, and will never be wrong. God made you and He has the manual on how to fix you.

When the people of Israel complained about Moses and the Lord, poisonous snakes were sent among them. God told Moses to make a snake of brass and hang it on a pole, and anyone who was bitten should look at it and they would be healed. They were not to glance at it, but to gaze intently at the snake. All they had to do was look.

"So Moses made the replica, and whenever anyone who had been bitten looked at the bronze snake, he recovered!"
(Numbers 21:9, TLB)

That snake represented Jesus. Why a snake and not a lamb? Jesus, although He had never sinned, received in His body our sin and fully paid for it. He allowed our sin to be put upon His body and He paid for every gross sin that was ever committed; He paid the full ransom needed to buy us back.

> *"For God took the sinless Christ and poured into him our sins. Then, in exchange, he poured God's goodness into us!"* *(2 Corinthians 5:21, TLB)*

Do you see that the people who had been bitten didn't have to do anything else but gaze intently at the brazen snake? They were not to pay attention to anything else. They didn't have to cry, scream, pray, or do penance. All they had to do was look!

Glory to God! You and I will make it, too! We will look to the Lamb who became that snake on the pole for us so that we could be healed. God does not change. He is the same yesterday, today, and forever.

You don't have to read your Bible for hours, pray in tongues for days, meditate, and fast. Nothing is wrong with doing all of that, but to be healed, all you have to do is look. Look to the Sacrifice for our sin, which is Jesus Christ our Savior. You are not to pay attention to the pain, the report of the doctor, the results of the tests, or a report of someone with the same symptoms who died. Your job is to keep your eyes focused on Him.

Remember that in the gospels, when Peter took his eyes off Jesus, he began to sink.

God sent His Word to heal you and He always keeps His Word. His Word works! Your healing may be instant or it may take some time before you can see and feel the total physical effects of God's healing power. Do not let doubts and lingering symptoms discourage you because you don't see immediate results. After all, when you go to a doctor, do you immediately feel better? No, the medication given to you usually takes some time before it begins to work. In the same way, the effects of divine healing may not appear instantly. It may take time for you to 'feel' completely healed.

Healing starts within and works out.

So what do you do in the meantime?

- Make God's Word the final authority. By His stripes you were healed (1 Peter 2:24).
- Refuse to believe what you see and feel. Only believe God's Word.
- Meditate on God's Word. Keep your mind fixed on the promises.
- Cast your care on the Lord. The devil will try to use anxiety over your situation to choke the Word out of your heart so that the promises will become unfruitful (Mark 4:19).
- Praise God for your healing. Praising God before you see a manifestation is the highest form of faith.
- Don't waver. Jesus said the person who wavers in his faith should not expect to receive anything from the Lord (James 1:6-7).
- Never let go! No matter what happens, continue to stand on God's Word for your healing.
- Listen to the Word. One of the main ways of keeping your mind renewed is to listen to it on audio or video, or say it to yourself out loud. Faith comes by 'hearing'.
- Confess the Word concerning your healing. Don't talk about your sickness. Speak only words that are in agreement with God's will for your healing.

Your Healing Prayer and Confession

Heavenly Father, I thank You for Your Word which says that by His stripes I was healed. I choose to believe Your healing power went to work in my body the instant hands were laid on me. That is the moment I believed Your Word. I confess Jesus Christ as Lord over my life—spirit, soul, and body. I have received the power of God to make me sound, whole, delivered, saved, and healed. Sickness, disease, and pain, I resist you in the name of Jesus. You are not the will of God for my life. I enforce the Word of God on you. I will not tolerate you in my life. My days of sickness and disease are over. Jesus bore my sickness, weakness, and pain. I am forever free! Father, thank You for watching over Your Word to perform it on my behalf. I praise You and bless You, in Jesus' name. (Isaiah 53:4-5, Psalm 103:1-5, Psalm 138:8, Romans 8:11)

What About When Symptoms Return?

Satan will always come back with symptoms and, if you agree with him, you will continue to be sick. It may take him years to come, but he will come. So don't ever say, 'I thought I was healed, but I guess I wasn't!' If symptoms return, stand against them. Say, 'No, you don't! I was healed at the cross, and I will stay healed.' Pick up your hammer (the Word of God) and hit those symptoms with what the Word says about the situation!

I had pernicious anemia when I was a very young girl. I had to have a transfusion once because my blood count was so low. When I was saved, I went to the Lord and received a manifested healing. Nineteen years later I went to a doctor for a checkup and the nurse told me I was anemic; I told her I couldn't be. She asked why and I told her that I was healed nineteen years ago and I was still healed. I remember her telling me that she didn't want to burst my faith bubble, but 'you are anemic'! She told me to fast for 12 hours and come back and they would tell me what medication I would have to take.

I went to a prayer group I was teaching that night and said, 'Lay your hands on me, not for healing, but to agree with me that I was healed nineteen years ago and I am still healed.' They did, and when I went back for the tests the following day, my blood count had jumped six points overnight.

I learned some things through that. You must stand your ground. Tell the enemy, 'No way, buster! I received my healing at Calvary and you have no right to steal it from me. Get out in the name of Jesus!' Fight the good fight of faith; it is a fight that has already been won.

'So, having done all to stand, stand therefore!' Jesus did all the work, and you get all the blessings. Always remember that Satan comes immediately to try to steal the word that was sown in your heart, but you don't have to let him take it away from you. Fight back! Stand!

> *"And these are the ones by the wayside where the word is*
> *sown. When they hear, Satan comes immediately and takes*
> *away the word that was sown in their hearts"*
> *(Mark 4:15, NKJV)*

Sometimes we may feel discouraged during the process of healing because it has not come as fast as we might like. We really don't know why some healings manifest immediately and why some take longer.

One possibility may be that the delay is because God's love for us is greater than an immediate 'fix'. He knows that if we did not really take the time to deal with the roots of the disease it would come back on us. That's when the 'Accuser of the Brethren' would come to us to accuse God and try to separate us from His love. God wants us to be firmly rooted in the truth of His Word so that the enemy will not have an open door to come and attack us with something worse.

Lies About God and Healing

Lie #1: God doesn't heal any more.

Lie #2: You never know whether it is God's will to heal or not.

Lie #3: God will make you sick to teach you something.

Lie #4: God was talking about spiritual healing when He said, 'By His stripes you were healed' in Isaiah 53.

Lie #5: Sometimes God says 'yes', sometimes He says 'no', and sometimes He says 'maybe'.

Let's dispel the lies once and for all by examining each of them according to the Word of God.

Lie #1:
God doesn't heal any more

> *"For I am the LORD, I change not; therefore ye sons of Jacob are not consumed."*
> *(Malachi 3:6)*

> *"Jesus Christ the same yesterday, and today, and for ever."*
> *(Hebrews 13:8)*

Praise God, He is still the same and still in the healing business! He does not change.

Lie #2:
You can never know if it is God's will to heal you or not

> *"And, behold, there came a leper and worshipped him, saying, Lord, if thou wilt, thou canst make me clean. And Jesus put forth his hand, and touched him, saying, I will; be thou clean. And immediately his leprosy was cleansed."*
> *(Matthew 8:2-3)*

If He ever said 'I will' to anyone, He is saying that to you. He is no respecter of persons. So if anyone is going to be healed, it might as well be you. You are a covenant child of God.

> *"Then Peter opened his mouth, and said, Of a truth I perceive that God is no respecter of persons"*
> *(Acts 10:34)*

Lie #3:
God will make you sick to teach you something

In the first place, God is not the author of sickness. Then there is the fact that God won't borrow something from Satan, the one who kills, steals, and destroys, to teach you something.

> *"But when He, the Spirit of Truth (the Truth-giving Spirit) comes, He will guide you into all the Truth (the whole, full Truth). For He will not speak His own message [on His own authority]; but He will tell whatever He hears [from the Father; He will give the message that has been given to Him], and He will announce and declare to you the things that are to come [that will happen in the future]."*
> *(John 16:13, AMP)*

Do you see that the Holy Spirit is our teacher? He does not use sickness to teach you anything. Now, don't get me wrong, you will learn some things through being sick, but there is a better way.

Can God use sickness to our advantage? You bet He can—God is so economical that He will not waste anything. If Satan tries to pull a fast one on you, God will turn it around and use it for your good. Try to keep a good attitude, pray in the Spirit and stand on the Word of God. God is for you, not against you.

Also, I advise you to never give credit to a sickness for the healing of another. What I mean by that is that some people have told me, 'I am so thankful for the heart attack I had, because when they treated me for that, they found I had cancer. If I hadn't had a heart attack, they wouldn't have found the cancer, and it might have killed me before I realized I had it.' It is God who gives us good things. Give God the glory for the healing and no credit for what Satan attempted to do to you.

> *"Every good gift and every perfect gift is from above, and comes down from the Father . . ."*
> *(James 1:17, NKJV)*

Give God the praise that they found the cancer; don't give the glory to anything else other than God and His goodness.

"And we know that God causes everything to work together for the good of those who love God and are called according to his purpose for them."
(Romans 8:28, NLT)

That verse in Romans 8 has been so misused. It has been used to justify a person's lack of faith, and their lack of fighting against whatever the devil sends. Just whatever will be will be; roll over and let the enemy wipe the floor up with you. ABSOLUTELY NOT!

Luke 10:19 tells us that God has given us authority and power over whatever comes at us. It is up to us to use that authority. Just know that the enemy puts up a great fight. You are going to need wisdom from God to be able to stand in this evil day.

A lady came and talked to me in a hushed tone of voice. She said, 'I want to tell you something.' I said, 'Ok, what is it?' She said, 'Two years ago the doctor told me I had breast cancer and needed to have my breast taken off in order to live.' I asked, 'What did you do?' She said, 'I never went back, I just prayed and did what I knew to do and all the symptoms left me.' She didn't become afraid. She didn't cry and tell everyone she talked to what the doctor said. She just went home and prayed and did what she knew to do. We need to be wise. **I am in *no way* telling you to *not* go to a doctor or *not* do what he says.** I am just letting you know that you should go to God first and do what He tells you to do. I know a lady who was told by the doctor that she had diabetes. She said, 'I just left that diagnosis with the doctor. I did not take it home with me.' That was years ago and she is still free from that disease. Learn a lesson: don't take that stuff home with you.

Your doctor is a practitioner. He is practicing medicine. He does not have all the answers, unless God gives them to him. We have a doctor, whose name is Jesus, and He has never lost a patient. God may want you to go to a doctor, but talk to God first before you go. And don't blindly do everything that a doctor may tell you to do. Ask God first before you take medicine or have an operation. Before you go to a doctor, ask God to guide you to the doctor of His choosing.

I wish to stress, *I am not against doctors.* Thank God for doctors! I have a doctor that I go to when the need arises. Some of us would have died before developing our faith enough to receive our healing if we hadn't gone to the doctor. I also go to a dentist two times a year to have my teeth cleaned. That is not a lack of faith. God is not against doctors. He gave us doctors, dentists, chiropractors, and other specialists as gifts for us to use as we need them. It is not a sin to visit a doctor. I am just telling you not to put your faith in the doctors. Put your faith in the Lord Jesus Christ and allow Him to work through the doctors, medicines, and technology.

Sometimes a person won't go to a doctor because they are afraid of what the doctor may tell them. I have known people who would possibly be alive today had they visited a doctor. They told me they were afraid the doctor would put fear in them. What they didn't realize was that they already had fear in them. You are not in faith if you are in fear. Go to God first and if your symptoms persist, find a competent doctor and find out what you are dealing with. If nothing else, you will be more equipped to know what you are praying against. You will not get healed by denying your symptoms!

Begin to take the Word of God like medicine. Meditate on the Scriptures until they become more real to you than the symptoms or the situation in your life. Use faith whether you are believing on your own, or whether you get help from a doctor. Use the physician's knowledge and your faith, and allow God to take you on your pathway to healing.

Keith Moore, a pastor who taught the Healing School at Rhema Bible Training Center in Tulsa, OK, tells of an incident where a man came to the Healing School with a large inoperable tumor on his brain. The doctors had told him that the roots from the tumor had gone so far down into the man's brain that it would kill him if they operated. The man attended Healing School every day for several weeks. He then went back to the surgeon and the doctor agreed to perform the operation. After the surgery, the surgeon reported that the roots of that tumor had shriveled up, and in surgery he just reached in and took the tumor out, and the man later recovered.

A friend of mine and I prayed for a lady who had a tumor in her uterus. She asked us to pray and we did. There was no visible evidence of healing, but when she went home, the tumor fell out on the floor.

Lie #4:
Those stripes were for spiritual healing
The stripes put on Jesus' back were physical stripes put there for your physical healing. When you were saved, God didn't give you a new body, but a new spirit and it does not need healing.

> *"Therefore if any person is [ingrafted] in Christ (the Messiah) he is a new creation (a new creature altogether); the old [previous moral and spiritual condition] has passed away. Behold, the fresh and new has come!"*
> *(2 Corinthians 5:17, AMP)*

Lie #5:
Sometimes God will say 'yes', sometimes He will say 'no', and sometimes He will say 'maybe'

> *"For all the promises of God in him are yea, and in him Amen, unto the glory of God by us."*
> *(2 Corinthians 1:20)*

If you can find a promise in the Word of God, God will never say no to it. He says yes to all of His promises.

Lies the Devil Will Tell You

'You have not prayed enough!', 'You have not fasted enough!', 'You have not confessed enough!' I have already stated that you cannot perform enough to deserve healing. You just need to receive what has already been done for you by Jesus.

You don't deserve healing!

Praise the Lord, I don't get what I deserve. I get what Jesus paid for. And if you want to examine closely what was done at the cross, you will find that I do deserve it. The newly born-again spirit man inside of me has done nothing wrong.

> *"Whosoever is born of God doth not commit sin; for his seed remaineth in him: and he cannot sin, because he is born of God."* (1 John 3:9)

I realize that if you are religious, you will have a problem with what I just said. But I didn't say it! It came from the Word of God. Check the Word out for yourself. Do not base what you believe on a preconceived idea, or what you have always thought. Study the Word and ask God what is true. Do not trust what you believe on what some denomination or a well-meaning preacher or scholar has said.

When I go to God in repentance, God does not examine me. He examines my substitute, Jesus. Just like in the Old Testament, when an Israelite took a lamb to the high priest to cover his sins, the high priest did not examine the man. The man had to bring a lamb without spot or blemish as a sacrifice.

The man came for forgiveness because he had spots, because he had missed the mark. The priest took the lamb and examined it. If the lamb was blemish free, the man laid his hands on the lamb and his sins were transferred to the lamb, and the forgiveness was passed on to the man. My High Priest is without spot or blemish, a perfect Lamb. He took my sin and transferred to me His righteousness. I can go away forgiven.

*"For by a single offering He has forever completely cleansed
and perfected those who are consecrated and made holy."
(Hebrews 10:14, AMP)*

*"Not by works of righteousness which we have done, but
according to his mercy he saved us, by the washing of
regeneration, and renewing of the Holy Ghost."
(Titus 3:5)*

*"For by grace are ye saved through faith; and that not of
yourselves: it is the gift of God: Not of works, lest any man
should boast."
(Ephesians 2:8-9)*

This is why I can say I am righteous and can receive healing.

We are Being Changed!

God's Word says we are being changed from glory to glory. What
does this mean? It means that day by day we are being changed
to be more like Him. Day by day, His love for us is transforming
us into His own image. Day by day, our born-again spirit is being
made alive in Christ Jesus. If you are considering what that looks
like, go to Galatians 5:22 and read about the fruits of the Spirit.

Let me tell you a little bit about how God has changed me. I came
from a broken home; my dad ran away and left us when I was only
two years old. I grew up angry and rebellious. I got married at
eighteen, had two children (who are my treasures), and was divorced
by twenty-five. I was determined to raise my children in a peaceful
home. I met my present husband when I was twenty-six and we
married in April of 1967. We both gave our hearts to the Lord that
November. Three years later we had a baby boy, who is another
one of my treasures from God. God delivered me from fear and
then began to work on my temper and attitude of rebellion. It took
years of taking the Word of God and letting Him work all the

anger and rebellion out of me. This is what the Lord Jesus is able to do for you. He can take a young, rebellious, angry, fearful little bit of a girl and turn her into a lady who loves people and loves God. He can use her to bring people to Jesus and see them healed and delivered. God gave us the peace in our home that I so desired for my family.

We should be full of patience. We should be full of peace. The fruits are the parts of God's nature that are being worked in us to reflect Him. When we face fear and defeat it, we bring glory to God. When we choose to like ourselves and defeat self-hatred, we bring glory to God. Step by step, glory to glory; each step, each new glory, is another victory for me and defeat for Satan!

Praise God today for His promise to change us into His very nature! Amen! Wherever we may be in our journey, remember that God hears our every prayer and He is faithful to complete the good work He has begun in us. We all have separate and unique journeys of healing.

Be encouraged today. God is meeting us one day at a time through His wisdom. Praise God now for all of His blessings and for sending the Holy Spirit to be our Comforter and Guide.

> *"But the Comforter, which is the Holy Ghost, whom the*
> *Father will send in my name, he shall teach you all things,*
> *and bring all things to your remembrance, whatsoever I have*
> *said unto you. Peace I leave with you, my peace I give unto*
> *you: not as the world giveth, give I unto you. Let not your*
> *heart be troubled, neither let it be afraid."*
> *(John 14:26-27)*

What About Paul's Thorn?

People have used Paul's thorn as an excuse to stay sick. They have said that Paul had an eye disease and that God told him that he would not be healed.

"But if ye will not drive out the inhabitants of the land from before you; then it shall come to pass, that those which ye let remain of them shall be pricks in your eyes, and thorns in your sides, and shall vex you in the land wherein ye dwell."
(Numbers 33:55)

"...even though I have received such wonderful revelations from God. So to keep me from becoming proud, I was given a thorn in my flesh, a messenger from Satan to torment me and keep me from becoming proud. Three different times I begged the Lord to take it away. Each time he said, 'My grace is all you need. My power works best in weakness.' So now I am glad to boast about my weaknesses, so that the power of Christ can work through me. That's why I take pleasure in my weaknesses, and in the insults, hardships, persecutions, and troubles that I suffer for Christ. For when I am weak, then I am strong."
(2 Corinthians 12:7-10, NLT)

"See with what large letters I have written to you with my own hand!"
(Galatians 6:11 NKJV)

Scholars and religious people have taught that God put an eye disease on Paul to keep him humble, and that when Paul asked Him to remove it, God said no. They have said that Paul had to write in large letters because the infection in his eyes was so bad that it made his eyes extremely watery. They use Galatians 4:15 as proof.

"Where is then the blessedness ye spake of? for I bear you record, that, if it had been possible, ye would have plucked out your own eyes, and have given them to me."
(Galatians 4:15)

In the first place, the Bible does not say that the thorn in the flesh was an eye disease. In the Old Testament, God told the twelve tribes of Israel to drive out the inhabitants of the Promised Land, and that if they didn't the inhabitants would be thorns in their flesh. He always referred to thorns in the flesh as people or demons.

He called Paul's thorn a 'messenger' of Satan sent to buffet him. Every place that Paul went there were people who were sent there to stir up trouble against him. I believe that was the 'messenger of Satan'.

I believe God was saying to Paul, 'I have given you the authority to get rid of this situation and my grace is sufficient for you.' I do not see a place in the Bible that says Paul had an eye disease. The Bible says he was blinded after meeting with Jesus on the road to Damascus, but it does not say he had an eye disease.

> *"Now as he traveled on, he came near to Damascus, and suddenly a light from heaven flashed around him. And he fell to the ground. Then he heard a voice saying to him, Saul, Saul, why are you persecuting Me [harassing, troubling, and molesting Me]? Then Saul got up from the ground, but though his eyes were opened, he could see nothing; so they led him by the hand and brought him into Damascus. And he was unable to see for three days, and he neither ate nor drank [anything].*
> *(Acts 9:3-4, 8-9, AMP)*

In Galatians 4, Paul talked about his temptation in his flesh. He was talking about something physical he had wrong with him and he called it a temptation in his flesh.

> *"And my temptation which was in my flesh ye despised not, nor rejected; but received me as an angel of God, even as Christ Jesus."*
> *(Galatians 4:14)*

I refuse to allow a false teaching about some perceived eye disease to keep me from being healed. So please don't allow some religious teaching about Paul having an eye disease to keep you from receiving what Jesus has for you. Even if Paul had a disease of the eyes, the Bible says that Jesus took our diseases and bore our sicknesses. I can see by what Jesus did for me that I don't have to be sick or have some disease regardless of who doesn't receive healing.

How About Job's Troubles?

People have taught on Job's sufferings as an excuse to stay sick. I have heard people say, 'I am suffering like Job, I am just like Job.' If you want to be like Job, you will end up healed and with twice as much as you had before.

> "And the Lord turned the captivity of Job and restored his fortunes, when he prayed for his friends; also the Lord gave Job twice as much as he had before."
> (Job 42:10, AMP)

> "One day the members of the heavenly court came to present themselves before the LORD, and the Accuser, Satan, came with them. 'Where have you come from?' the LORD asked Satan. Satan answered the LORD, 'I have been patrolling the earth, watching everything that's going on.' Then the LORD asked Satan, 'Have you noticed my servant Job? He is the finest man in all the earth. He is blameless—a man of complete integrity. He fears God and stays away from evil.' Satan replied to the LORD, 'Yes, but Job has good reason to fear God. You have always put a wall of protection around him and his home and his property. You have made him prosper in everything he does. Look how rich he is! But reach out and take away everything he has and he will surely curse you to your face!' 'All right, you may test him,' the LORD said to Satan. 'Do whatever you want with everything he possesses, but don't harm him physically.' So

Satan left the LORD's presence. One day when Job's sons and daughters were feasting at the oldest brother's house, a messenger arrived at Job's home with this news: 'Your oxen were plowing, with the donkeys feeding beside them, when the Sabeans raided us. They stole all the animals and killed all the farmhands. I am the only one who escaped to tell you.' While he was still speaking, another messenger arrived with this news: 'The fire of God has fallen from heaven and burned up your sheep and all the shepherds. I am the only one who escaped to tell you.' While he was still speaking, a third messenger arrived with this news: 'Three bands of Chaldean raiders have stolen your camels and killed your servants. I am the only one who escaped to tell you.' While he was still speaking, another messenger arrived with this news: 'Your sons and daughters were feasting in their oldest brother's home. Suddenly, a powerful wind swept in from the wilderness and hit the house on all sides. The house collapsed, and all your children are dead. I am the only one who escaped to tell you.'"
(Job 1:6-19, NLT)

As you read this passage for yourself you will find that it was the devil that attacked Job. It was not God. God did use Job's experience to teach him and his friends—and us—something. There are no discrepancies in the Word and no mistakes. If something sounds like it goes against the nature of God, go back and read it again.

Job still had a hedge of protection around him, but Satan was allowed to attack Job. He had a hedge about him, but Job didn't know that. We have that same protection in the Word, but some of us don't know it. We don't take the time to find out what belongs to us within the Word of God.

A Curse Causeless

"As the bird by wandering, as the swallow by flying, so the

curse causeless shall not come."
(Proverbs 26:2)

The curse does not come without a reason, but I don't have to try and figure out what that reason is. Don't listen to the devil's lies. I know Jesus paid for whatever the curse is. All I have to do is take responsibility for the sin that opened the door, confess it, and close that door. I then cover that door with the blood of Jesus and go on from there.

We are not responsible for the sins of our fathers, but someone opened the door to that iniquity allowing some things we don't want to affect our DNA. That bend of iniquity came in, and if I will take responsibility for that thing that opened the door, I can then break that thing off my lineage.

Remember, you are not called to be a 'gap-finder'. You are a 'gap-stander'; we are called to stand in the gap for those who are weak. We are not to point out their faults and accuse them. Jesus always stands with the accused, not the accuser!

There is MUCH power in the precious blood of Jesus.

"The blood shall be to you for a token [or sign to you] upon the houses where ye are: and when I see the blood, I will pass over you, and the plague shall not be upon you to destroy you, when I smite the land of Egypt. The LORD *will pass over the door and will not suffer the destroyer to come in unto your houses to smite you."*
(Exodus 12:13a, 23b)

My Affirmation of the Word

Jesus, I take Your precious blood and apply it to the door through which this infirmity came in. I bind you, Satan, and command you to take your hands off my body. Your assignment is cancelled and I break your power over me and my family, in the name of Jesus. Thank You, Father, that the curse is now broken and I, and my seed, are set free from this sickness.

Now, in agreement with you, I declare you to be set free and believe that the Word of God is now working in your life to keep you healed. Father, You sent Your Word and healed them and delivered them from all their destructions, and now we have a new and better covenant based on new and better promises. I thank You for the work You have done on Calvary to provide for our deliverance and healing. I love You, Jesus, and will be eternally grateful for all You have done.

Erroneous Belief Systems

Most people's belief system is based on what has happened to them or to someone they know. They do not establish their belief on what the Word says.

For example: Grandma was a great lady who loved God with all her heart; she was at church every time the doors were open, she helped everyone she could, she worked at the church all the time, yet she got sick and died. If God were to heal anyone, it surely would have been her. People base what they believe on what happened to Grandma, when the Word clearly states that He bore our sins and carried our diseases. Do not make a doctrine out of any circumstance in your life.

A well-meaning preacher once told me, 'If God was going to heal anyone it would have been my dad. He was such a great man and people all over the world were praying for him. Since he died, it is not God's will to heal anymore.' He based what he believed on what happened to his earthly father. That is poor ground to stand on.

I tell you again, 'Your good works cannot get you healed.' Only your faith in what Jesus accomplished.

Always ask yourself this, 'What does the Word say?' Get to know the Word of God. I cannot stress this enough! God only speaks the Word. That is the language He speaks.

I had a person tell me once that God 'told her' that He had put a sickness on her, but He was about to take it off when she learned what she was supposed to learn from this trial. Listen very carefully and learn this: God will NEVER tell you anything contrary to His Word.

"For the Word that God speaks is alive and full of power [making it active, operative, energizing, and effective]; it is sharper than any two-edged sword, penetrating to the dividing line of the breath of life (soul) and [the immortal] spirit, and of joints and marrow [of the deepest parts of our nature], exposing and sifting and analyzing and judging the very thoughts and purposes of the heart."
(Hebrews 4:12, AMP)

CHAPTER 5 NOTES AND REFLECTIONS

Chapter 6

HOW TO REVERSE THAT CURSE

1: Be convinced you are redeemed

Take a look in the mirror and tell yourself what Job proclaimed: 'I know that my Redeemer lives' (Job 19:25). We are also reminded in Galatians 3:13 that Christ redeemed us. Ephesians 1:7 tells us that we have redemption through His blood.

2: Declare who you are in Christ

Psalm 107:2 says, 'Let the redeemed of the LORD say so!' You have to use your words to declare who you are. You are redeemed, so say it. Say it when you feel like it, and say it when you don't feel like it. **Use your words to direct the outcome of your life**. Proverbs 18:21 reminds us that life, blessing, and prosperity are in the power of your tongue.

3: Stop expecting bad things to happen to you

Sometimes we 'brace ourselves' for bad news and bad things so that they don't jolt us too much. Stop conditioning yourself to expect negative things to happen. Your spirit has enough energy and chemistry in it to bring those things upon you. That's what Job meant when he said, 'What I feared has come upon me' (Job 3:25, NIV).

4: Give a sacrificial gift

When you bring a sacrificial gift to God, it is not as if God needs it—**but you do**! Your gift or your seed releases your faith to have God involved in your situation. REMEMBER THIS SPIRITUAL KEY TO VICTORY!

"Will a man rob God? Yet ye have robbed me. But ye say, wherein have we robbed thee? In tithes and offerings. Ye are cursed with a curse: for ye have robbed me, even this whole nation. Bring ye all the tithes into the storehouse, that there may be meat in mine house, and prove me now herewith, saith the LORD of hosts, if I will not open you the windows of heaven, and pour you out a blessing, that there shall not be room enough to receive it. And I will rebuke the devourer for your sakes, and he shall not destroy the fruits of your ground; neither shall your vine cast her fruit before the time in the field, saith the LORD of hosts."
(Malachi 3:8-11)

"But unto you that fear my name shall the Sun of righteousness arise with healing in his wings; and ye shall go forth, and grow up as calves of the stall."
(Malachi 4:2)

Do you see how important the tithe is where your healing is concerned?

You can get healed because you tithe, you can get your kids saved because you tithe.

5: You need to understand how important your words really are

Say what the Father says about you. He declares you're healed by the stripes of Jesus. When you state, 'I will', this is the strongest assertion that can be made in the English language. When you boldly speak the Word of God and make the following confessions in regards to your healing (or whatever it is you are asking God for), believe you have received. God has already said, '*I will* take sickness away from the midst of you,' so count it as done.

> *"Brood of vipers! How can you, being evil, speak good things? For out of the abundance of the heart the mouth speaks. For by your words you will be justified, and by your words you will be condemned."*
> *(Matthew 12:34, 37, NKJV)*

> *"The tongue can bring death or life; those who love to talk will reap the consequences."*
> *(Proverbs 18:21, NLT)*

> *"Whosoever therefore shall confess me before men, him will I confess also before my Father which is in heaven. But whosoever shall deny me before men, him will I also deny before my Father which is in heaven."*
> *(Matthew 10:32-33)*

> *"I tell you the truth, everyone who acknowledges me publicly here on earth, the Son of Man will also acknowledge in the presence of God's angels."*
> *(Luke 12:8, NLT)*

We really do need to see how very important our words are. They are either words of faith or fear. **Choose wisely**!

The Word of God and the Son of God are the same. Anything Jesus can do, His Word can do. Every Word has the power to bring itself to pass.

> *"He is dressed in a robe dyed by dipping in blood, and the title by which He is called is The Word of God."*
> *(Revelation 19:13, AMP)*

"In the beginning [before all time] was the Word (Christ) and the Word was with God, and the Word was God Himself."
(John 1:1, AMP)

Do you see that the Word and Jesus are the same? Jesus is called the Word. So you can see how important the Word of God is?

"For as [surely as] the earth brings forth its shoots, and as a garden causes what is sown in it to spring forth, so [surely] the Lord God will cause rightness and justice and praise to spring forth before all the nations [through the self-fulfilling power of His word]."
(Isaiah 61:11, AMP)

"For with God nothing is ever impossible and no word from God shall be without power or impossible of fulfillment."
(Luke 1:37, AMP)

"For the Word that God speaks is alive and full of power [making it active, operative, energizing, and effective]; it is sharper than any two-edged sword, penetrating to the dividing line of the breath of life (soul) and [the immortal] spirit, and of joints and marrow [of the deepest parts of our nature], exposing and sifting and analyzing and judging the very thoughts and purposes of the heart."
(Hebrews 4:12, AMP)

"For as the rain and snow come down from the heavens, and return not there again, but water the earth and make it bring forth and sprout, that it may give seed to the sower and bread to the eater, So shall My Word be that goes forth out of My mouth: it shall not return to Me void [without producing any effect, useless], but it shall accomplish that which I please and purpose, and it shall prosper in the thing for which I sent it."
(Isaiah 55:10-11, AMP)

I'll say it again: whatever Jesus can do, the Word of God can do. We have to take the Word and put it to work in our lives, saying the same thing Jesus said in His Word.

> *"And they have overcome (conquered) him by means of the blood of the Lamb and by the utterance of their testimony, for they did not love and cling to life even when faced with death [holding their lives cheap till they had to die for their witnessing]." (Revelation 12:11, AMP)*

Let's imagine this:

Satan goes before the Lord accusing us of all kinds of things. When you want a healing, the prosecuting attorney, Satan, goes before God, the Judge, stating all the reasons why we should not be healed. Jesus, our attorney, says, 'Father, I took the stripes on My back to pay for the defendant's healing.' The Judge asks, 'Do You have any witnesses?' He says, 'Yes Sir, I call the Blood to the stand.' The Blood says, 'I paid for their healing when the stripes were put on Jesus' back.' The Bible says that out of the mouth of three or four witnesses a thing shall be established. The Judge asks, 'Do You have another witness?'

That is the place where you have to agree with your attorney and not the prosecuting attorney. You overcome by the Blood of the Lamb and the words of your testimony. You don't want to say, 'I know I have blown it and am not worthy to be healed.' You must say what your attorney says: 'By the stripes of Jesus I am healed. I have a right to be healed because of what Jesus did for me.' The judge says, 'Case dismissed! Amen!'

A Confession for a Long and Healthy Life

I confess that I will live strong and be satisfied with long life. All my arteries and veins are clear and free from blockages. Dementia, Alzheimer's and memory loss have no place in my life. I have the mind of Christ and my memory is blessed. I remember names, dates, people, places, and events. I declare that signs of old age do not belong in my body, and I tell them to get out, in the name of Jesus.

My joints are healthy and I have no loss of cartilage. I do not require replacements of any kind. The veins in my extremities are healthy and free from clots and blockages. My feet are healthy and without defect. I do not have bunions, corns, or any other problems with my feet.

I am free of pains, lumps, age spots, and any other thing that time tries to put on me. I have skin like a baby with no blemishes or wrinkles.

My hormones are like those of a young person. I do not have viruses or funguses living in my body. My kidneys, liver, bladder, lungs, brain, and all other organs function properly. My heart was made to last one hundred and twenty years and I tell it to beat properly. My eyes see perfectly with twenty/twenty vision and with no defects. My ears are clear to hear with no loss of hearing. I have a full head of healthy hair for God has counted the exact number. My teeth, gums, tongue, and mouth are healthy and clean and without disease.

My body does not respond to condemnation and shame or guilt. I have the same Holy Ghost renewal in my body that Abraham and Sarah had in theirs. God has made me beautiful. I am fearfully and wonderfully made. I love the Lord with all my heart and will use the good life He gives me to glorify Him. I will be a good example to others on how to live for my Savior. I will not wear out, give out, burn out, or quit. I will go home to be with Jesus at a ripe old age with all my parts still working. I will always be able to take care of my personal needs.

Now as you speak these words of confession over your life, healing and health become yours. You are protecting your healing and health. God's Word becomes your healing. It becomes whatever we need it to be.

God sent forth Jesus who went about teaching, preaching, and healing the sick. Anybody who believes that He was sent from God, and puts faith in His Words will be healed. I want you to put your faith in the words written above and believe that the Spirit of God has set it up so that you can read this book, and that the anointing is present to set you free. I offer this prayer to set you free and agree for your healing.

Father, I pray in the name of Jesus that You would touch the ones reading this and set them free from disease. I rebuke sickness in the name of Jesus and I declare the Word of God and the blood of Jesus to be in control here. I bind the spirit of infirmity and call it out in Jesus' name. Your Word says that by Your stripes they are healed. You took our sicknesses and bore away our diseases. You were wounded for our transgressions, You were bruised for our iniquities, the chastisement of our peace was upon You, and by Your stripes we are healed and made whole. Amen!

CHAPTER 6 NOTES AND REFLECTIONS

Chapter 7

DIPLOMATIC IMMUNITY

A person born in the United States of America has certain rights as a citizen. If a person is a guest from another country, they must abide by the laws of this land. However, if they are a diplomat from another country and commit a crime, the United States government does not have the right to punish them: they have 'diplomatic immunity'. The U.S. government will deport them out of this country and send them back to their homeland, where it becomes the responsibility of the country they came from to deal with their crime.

When I was talking to the Lord about being His ambassador, He told me that I have diplomatic immunity. We are only ambassadors to this world; this is not our permanent home.

> *"We are therefore Christ's ambassadors, as though God were making his appeal through us. We implore you on Christ's behalf: Be reconciled to God."*
> *(2 Corinthians 5:20, NIV)*

Just as the diplomat from another country represents the opinion of the country from which they came, you, as an ambassador of God's kingdom, must not have another opinion except the one that represents your 'country'. The country you come out of is responsible for supplying food, clothing, shelter, and any other need you may have while you are away from your home. The country you came out of, the Kingdom of God, says, 'By His stripes you are healed' (Isaiah 53:4-5). The body has to line up with the opinion of its homeland. If a crime is committed by you while you are a resident in a foreign land (the world), as an ambassador of heaven this world system, or the ruler of this world, does not have the right to punish you.

> *"...in which you used to live when you followed the ways of this world and of the ruler of the kingdom of the air, the spirit who is now at work in those who are disobedient."*
> *(Ephesians 2:2, NIV)*

You must be sent back to the country you represent. I represent the Kingdom of God and, as its ambassador, I am the responsibility of God the Father. It is His responsibility to discipline me. He has already put my punishment on His Son, Jesus Christ. God will deal with me as His child—as a father disciplines his children, God will chastise me.

> *"For whom the Lord loveth he chasteneth, and scourgeth every son whom he receiveth."*
> *(Hebrews 12:6)*

The word 'chastise' means to child train. I am here to tell you that my punishment will not be cancer, diabetes, or some other ungodly disease from the pit. God said He sent the Holy Spirit to teach me all things. My Father will not use some sickness or disease to teach me anything. The Holy Spirit will guide me into all truth.

I am not saying it is a good thing to commit crimes or do other wrong things. We know from the Word of God that it is wrong to do such things. I am underlining the fact that Jesus paid for all my sins and that He took upon His precious back the stripes that made me whole. Therefore, the enemy of my soul does not have legal rights to lay sickness or disease, torment or mental pressure, on my person.

"He does not treat us as our sins deserve or repay us according to our iniquities."
(Psalm 103:10, NIV)

God will deal with me as His child. Are you beginning to see that the devil cannot do anything he desires to a child of God who knows who he is and what belongs to him?

"If we confess our sins, he is faithful and just to forgive us our sins, and to cleanse us from all unrighteousness."
(1 John 1:9)

Since Jesus paid for my sins and took care of the punishment due me, my sins are none of the devil's business. The devil cannot lay some sickness or disease on me unless I allow him to do so.

If through just being a part of a fallen world some disease shows up in my body, I have the authority as a child of God and as the righteousness of God in Christ to send it packing. I can tell the disease to leave my body and enforce what the Word of God says about it.

"The LORD will perfect that which concerneth me: thy mercy, O LORD, endureth for ever: forsake not the works of thine own hands."
(Psalm 138:8)

Begin to claim your diplomatic immunity.

Chapter 8

AFFIRMATIONS AND CONFESSIONS

I declare that I am in good health; I am alive. *(Genesis 43:28)*

He is the Lord that healed me. *(Exodus 15:26)*

I am blessed coming in and going out. I am blessed in my body. I serve the Lord and He blesses my bread and water, and He takes sickness away from the middle of me. *(Exodus 23:25)*

The Lord is taking all sickness away from me. *(Deuteronomy 7:15)*

You have set before me the way of life and the way of death. I will choose Your way and I shall live. *(Deuteronomy 30:19)*

You have redeemed my life from all adversity. *(2 Samuel 4:9)*

You do not take away life but devise ways so that I will be drawn in close to You. *(2 Samuel 14:14)*

I offer sacrifices of sweet savor unto God and pray for my life and the lives of my children. *(Ezra 6:10)*

If it pleases You and I have found favor in Your sight, let my life be given to me. *(Esther 7:3)*

I gather together with other believers and stand for my life. I destroy, slay, and cause to perish all the powers that would rise up to assault me. I take the spoil of them for prize. *(Esther 8:11)*

You have granted me life and favor, and Your care has preserved my spirit. *(Job 10:12)*

My life is brighter than the noonday. Though I was in darkness, I am like the morning. *(Job 11:17)*

My life and breath are in Your hands. *(Job 12:10)*

The Spirit of God has made me, and the Almighty gives me life. You keep my life from perishing. *(Job 33:4, 18)*

You will show me the path of life. *(Psalm 16:11)*

You meet me with blessings of goodness. You set a crown of pure gold upon my head. I asked You for my life, and You gave it to me. You gave me length of days forever and ever. *(Psalm 21:3-4)*

Goodness and mercy follow me all the days of my life, and I will dwell in the house of the Lord forever. *(Psalm 23:6)*

The Lord is the strength of my life. *(Psalm 27:1)*

I called to You, God, and You healed me. You kept me alive. Your favor is for my life. *(Psalm 30:2-3, 5)*

I desire life and to live many days that I may see good. Therefore, I will fear the Lord and keep my tongue from evil and my lips from speaking deceit. I will depart from evil and do good, seek peace and pursue it. *(Psalm 34:11-14)*

Let my enemy who seeks after my life be put to shame and brought to confusion. *(Psalm 35:4)*

Rescue me from destruction and my life from the lions. *(Psalm 35:17)*

You, O Lord, are my fountain of life. *(Psalm 36:9)*

I will praise Him who is the health of my countenance and my God. I refuse to be discouraged. I refuse to fear. *(Psalm 43:5)*

Your loving kindness is better than life, and my lips will praise You. I will bless You while I live. I will lift up my hands in Your name. *(Psalm 63:3-4)*

My life is preserved from fear of the enemy. *(Psalm 64:1)*

Let my enemy, who seeks to destroy my life, be ashamed and brought to mutual confusion. Let him be driven backward and brought to dishonor. *(Psalm 70:2)*

Preserve my life, for I am holy and You are my God. Save me because I trust in You. *(Psalm 86:2)*

I dwell in the secret place of the Most High, I rest in His shadow. *(Psalm 91:1-2)*

No evil will conquer me, no plague will come near me. *(Psalm 91:10)*

I call and You answer me. You are with me in trouble. You will deliver me and honor me. You will satisfy me with long life and show me Your salvation. *(Psalm 91:15-16)*

I will bless the Lord and will not forget His benefits. He has forgiven my sins and healed all my diseases. He has redeemed my life from destruction and crowned me with loving-kindness and tender mercies. God has satisfied me with good things, so that my youth is renewed like the eagles. *(Psalm 103:1-5)*

God has redeemed me out of the hand of the enemy and I say so. I am the redeemed of the Lord. God sent His Word and healed me and delivered me from all destruction. *(Psalm 107:2, 20)*

God is on my side; I choose not to fear. I shall not die, but live and declare the works of the Lord. *(Psalm 118:6, 17)*

My hope is in the Word You have spoken to me. It is a comfort in my affliction. Your Word has given me life. *(Psalm 119:49-50)*

I will not perish in my affliction because I delight in Your law. I will not forget Your precepts, for by them You have given me life. *(Psalm 119:92-93)*

I face Your Temple as I worship, giving thanks to You for all Your loving-kindness and Your faithfulness, for Your promises are backed by all the honor of Your name. God will perfect all the things that concern me. *(Psalm 138:2, 8)*

The fear of the Lord is health to my body and strength to my bones. *(Proverbs 3:7-8)*

I will give attention to the Words of God. I will incline my ear to His sayings. They will not depart from my eyes. I will keep them in the middle of my heart because they are life to me and health to my body. *(Proverbs 4:20-22)*

I will speak with wisdom and promote health. *(Proverbs 12:18)*

I will receive and speak only pleasant words. They are like a honeycomb; sweetness to my soul and health to my bones. *(Proverbs 16:24)*

You will restore me and make me live. *(Isaiah 38:16)*

Every day as I wait upon the Lord, He renews my strength. I will rise up as the eagles. I will run and not get weary. I will walk and not faint. *(Isaiah 40:31)*

His Word will not return void, but will accomplish what it was sent to do. *(Isaiah 55:11)*

The healing of the Lord will spring forth speedily. *(Isaiah 58:8)*

You have given my life to me as a prize in all places, wherever I go. *(Jeremiah 45:5)*

You have redeemed my life. *(Lamentations 3:58)*

You saw me polluted in my own blood and spoke to me and said, 'Live!' *(Ezekiel 16:6)*

I will surely live and not die because I walk in the statutes of life without committing iniquity. *(Ezekiel 33:15)*

You have brought my life up from the pit. *(Jonah 2:6)*

The Lord my God, in the middle of me, is mighty. He will save, He will rejoice over me with joy, and He will rest in His love for me. He will joy over me with singing. *(Zephaniah 3:17)*

Your covenant with me is one of life and peace. *(Malachi 2:5)*

I choose not to be offended and I am being delivered out of all afflictions and persecutions. *(Matthew 5:10-12)*

Speak a Word, Lord, and heal me this very hour. Jesus took my infirmities and bore my diseases. *(Matthew 8:8, 13, 17)*

I confess the Word of God before men and before my Father. *(Matthew 10:32)*

Jesus said if I can believe, all things are possible, so I believe. *(Mark 9:23)*

I have authority over the devil and no demon power can hurt me. *(Luke 10:19)*

I am a child of God, fully accepted by the Father. *(John 1:12)*

I will drink of the water you gave me so that I will never thirst again. The water you gave me will become to me a fountain of water springing up into everlasting life. *(John 4:13-14)*

I have everlasting life because I have heard Your Word and I believe in You. I have passed from death to life. *(John 5:24)*

Jesus, You are my Bread of Life. I will live forever because I eat of the living bread. *(John 6:48, 51)*

The Spirit gives me life. His Words are Spirit and life to me. *(John 6:63)*

Through You, I have life and life more abundantly. *(John 10:10)*

I have eternal life and will not perish. I will not be snatched out of the hand of God. *(John 10:28-29)*

I will live because I believe in Christ Jesus, who is the resurrection and the life. *(John 11:25-26)*

You are the Way, the Truth, and the Life. *(John 14:6)*

Jesus went about doing *good* and healing *all* that are oppressed of the devil. *(Acts 10:38)*

I am loved by God regardless of how I perform. *(Romans 5:8)*

I believe that the same Spirit that raised Jesus from the dead lives in me, and that He will quicken my mortal body. Therefore, I forbid my body to be sick. I tell my body it is healed and has to act like it. *(Romans 8:11)*

I have the wisdom of God; and righteousness, sanctification, and redemption by Him. *(1 Corinthians 1:30)*

I am set in the body of Christ and I know that I am valuable and important to the work of God. *(1 Corinthians 12:20-25)*

I believe, therefore I speak. I receive my healing. I don't consider what I feel, I believe I am healed. YOU HAVE HEALED ME! *(2 Corinthians 4:13)*

I am blessed and it's just a matter of time before things change. What I see now is only temporary. *(2 Corinthians 4:18)*

I am a new creature predestined for greatness. *(2 Corinthians 5:17)*

I am a giver and God is causing people to help me prosper. *(2 Corinthians 9:5)*

Christ has redeemed me from the curse of the law, having been made a curse for me. For it is written, cursed is everyone who hangs on a tree that the blessing of Abraham might come on me through Jesus, so that I might receive the promise of the Spirit through faith. *(Galatians 3:13-14)*

Since I belong to Christ, I am Abraham's seed and therefore I can have the promises Abraham received. *(Galatians 3:29)*

The Holy Spirit is my helper; I'm never alone and I have the peace of God. He keeps my heart and mind through Christ Jesus. *(Philippians 4:7)*

Jesus is the same yesterday, today, and forever. *(Hebrews 13:8)*

I am redeemed by the blood of the Lamb; that Lamb is Jesus. I believe in God through Jesus. Because God raised Jesus from the dead and gave Him glory, my faith and hope are in God. He saw the redeemed and raised up Jesus before the foundation of the world. *(1 Peter 1:18-21)*

I am healed by Your stripes and sickness will not lord over my body. *(1 Peter 2:24)*

I am forgiven and will not be tormented by past errors. *(1 John 1:9)*

I am an overcomer and my faith is changing my circumstances. *(1 John 5:4)*

I declare that I prosper in all things and am in good health, just as my soul prospers. *(3 John 2)*

I am built solid, grounded in righteousness,
far from any trouble—nothing to fear!
far from terror—it won't even come close!
If anyone attacks me,
I won't for a moment suppose that God sent them,
And if any should attack,
nothing will come of it.
God created the blacksmith
who fires up his forge
and makes a weapon designed to kill.
God also created the destroyer—
but no weapon that can hurt me has ever been forged.
Any accuser who takes me to court
will be dismissed as a liar.
This is what GOD's servants can expect.
God will *see to it that everything works out for the best.*
That is GOD's Decree.

I am the healed of God protecting my health by His Word.
I love God and will live each day for Him to the best of my ability.
I walk in health because I am a covenant child of God.

Confession to Live Healthy

Father, I commit to live a healthy lifestyle with your help. I will prepare healthy foods for my family and myself. I will treat my body like the Temple of the Holy Spirit and won't misuse it.

I refuse to eat foods that deplete my body of the essential nutrients it needs to prosper. This day I separate myself unto God, and I will only eat that which is good, healthy, and nutritional. I will exercise regularly so that my body is strong and limber, and I say I have excellent muscle tone and endurance. I enter into God's rest and will cease from my own works. My life is balanced according to God's perfect plan for me. I get sufficient rest and sleep like a baby.

I bring my body into subjection, and do not allow my flesh to control me. I am temperate in all things. I curse all destructive cravings for food and substances that threaten my health. I speak to all the junk food that tries to tempt me. I tell it, 'You have no power to control my desires or my appetite.' I declare I am free from all bondages to chocolate and sugar, and all unhealthy food products.

I draw from the wisdom of God to direct me to shop for healthy foods and to manage my time properly so that I don't fall back into bad eating habits. I tell my body to obey me and command my mind to focus on the things that will glorify God. I walk in the spirit and I will not fulfill the lusts of the flesh. I ask the Father to help me fulfill what I have promised here, in Jesus' name. Amen.

PERSONAL AFFIRMATIONS

Chapter 9

GOD'S OWN WORDS ON HEALING

Old Testament

Your days shall be 120 years. *(Genesis 6:3)*

You shall be buried in a good old age. *(Genesis 15:15)*

When I see the blood, I will pass over you, and the plague shall not be upon you to destroy you. *(Exodus 12:13)*

I am the Lord that heals you. *(Exodus 15:26)*

I will take sickness away from the midst of you and the number of your days I will fulfill. *(Exodus 23:25-26)*

I will keep you free from every disease. *(Deuteronomy 7:15)*

It will be well with you and your days shall be multiplied and prolonged as the days of heaven on earth. *(Deuteronomy 11:21)*

I turned the curse into a blessing unto you, because I loved you. *(Deuteronomy 23:5)*

I have redeemed you from every sickness and every plague. *(Deuteronomy 28:61)*

The joy of the Lord is your strength. *(Nehemiah 8:10)*

You shall come to your grave in a full age like as a shock of corn comes in its season. *(Job 5:26)*

I have found a ransom for you, your flesh shall be fresher than a child's, and you shall return to the days of your youth. *(Job 33:24-25)*

I will give you strength and bless you with peace. *(Psalm 29:11)*

I have healed you and brought up your soul from the grave; I have kept you alive from going down into the pit. *(Psalm 30:1-2)*

I will preserve you and keep you alive. *(Psalm 41:2)*

I will strengthen you upon the bed of languishing; I will turn all your bed in your sickness. *(Psalm 41:3)*

I am the health of your countenance and your God. *(Psalm 43:5)*

No plague shall come near your dwelling. *(Psalm 91:10)*

I will satisfy you with long life. *(Psalm 91:16)*

I heal all your diseases. *(Psalm 103:3)*

You are my redeemed—say so! *(Psalm 107:2)*

I sent my Word and healed you and delivered you from your destructions. *(Psalm 107:20)*

You shall not die, but live, and declare my works. *(Psalm 118:17)*

I heal your broken heart and bind up your wounds. *(Psalm 147:3)*

Trusting Me brings health to your navel and marrow to your bones. *(Proverbs 3:8)*

The years of your life shall be many. *(Proverbs 4:10)*

My words are life and health to all your flesh. *(Proverbs 4:22)*

My good report makes your bones fat. *(Proverbs 15:30)*

Pleasant words are life to you, and health/medicine to your bones. *(Proverbs 16:24)*

A merry heart does good like a medicine. *(Proverbs 17:22)*

The tongue of the dumb shall sing, the stammering tongue shall speak plainly. The eyes of the blind shall be opened. The ears of the deaf shall be unstopped. *(Isaiah 32:4-5)*

The eyes of them that see shall not be dim. The ears of them that hear shall hearken. The lame man shall leap as a hart. *(Isaiah 35:5-6)*

I will recover you and make you to live. I am ready to save you. *(Isaiah 38:16, 20)*

I give power to the faint. I increase strength to them that have no might. *(Isaiah 40:29, 31)*

I will strengthen and help you. You shall run and not grow weary, you shall walk and not faint. *(Isaiah 41:10)*

To your old age and gray hairs, I will carry you and I will deliver you. *(Isaiah 46:4)*

I carried your pains and with my stripes you are healed. *(Isaiah 53:5)*

I bore all your sickness; I was put to sickness for you. *(Isaiah 53:10)*

I will heal you. *(Isaiah 57:19)*

Your light shall break forth as the morning and your health shall spring forth speedily. *(Isaiah 58:8)*

I will restore health unto you, and I will heal you of your wounds saith the Lord. *(Jeremiah 30:17)*

Behold I will bring it health and cure, and I will cure you, and will reveal unto you the abundance of peace and truth. *(Jeremiah 33:6)*

I will bind up that which was broken and strengthen that which was sick. *(Ezekiel 34:16)*

Behold, I will cause breath to enter into you and you shall live. I shall put My Spirit in you and you shall live. *(Ezekiel 37:5, 14)*

Whithersoever the rivers shall come shall live. They shall be healed and everything shall live where the river comes. *(Ezekiel 47:9)*

Seek Me and you shall live. *(Amos 5:4, 6)*

I have arisen with healing in My wings. *(Malachi 4:2)*

New Testament
I will, be thou clean. *(Matthew 8:3)*

I took your infirmities and bore your sicknesses. *(Matthew 8:17)*

If you are sick, you need a physician. (I am the Lord your Physician.) *(Matthew 9:12)*

According to your faith, be it done unto you. *(Matthew 9:29)*

I give you authority to drive out evil spirits and to heal all manner of sickness and all manner of disease. *(Matthew 10:1)*

I heal them all. *(Matthew 12:15)*

I am moved with compassion toward the sick and I heal them. *(Matthew 14:14)*

As many as touch Me are made perfectly whole. *(Matthew 14:36)*

Every plant not planted by Me shall be uprooted. *(Matthew 15:13)*

Healing is the children's bread. *(Matthew 15:26)*

I do all things well. I make the deaf to hear and the dumb to speak. *(Mark 7:37)*

If you can believe, all things are possible to him that believes. *(Mark 9:23, 11:23-24)*

When hands are laid on you, you shall recover. *(Mark 16:18)*

My anointing heals the brokenhearted, and delivers the captives, recovers sight to the blind, and sets at liberty those who are bruised. *(Luke 4:18)*

Daughter, your faith in Me has healed you. Go in peace. *(Luke 8:48)*

I heal all those who have need of healing. *(Luke 9:11)*

I am not come to destroy men's lives but to save them. *(Luke 9:56)*

Behold I give you authority over all the enemy's power and nothing shall by any means hurt you. *(Luke 10:19)*

Sickness is satanic bondage and you ought to be loosed today. *(Luke 18; 2 Corinthians 6:2)*

In Me is life. *(John 1:4)*

I am the Bread of Life. I give you life. *(John 6:33, 35)*

The words I speak unto you are Spirit and Life. *(John 6:63)*

I am come that you might have life, and that you might have it more abundantly. *(John 10:10)*

I am the resurrection and the life. *(John 11:25)*

If you ask anything in My name, I will do it. *(John 14:14)*

Faith in My name makes you strong and gives you perfect soundness. *(Acts 3:16)*

I stretch forth My hand to heal. *(Acts 4:30)*

I, Jesus Christ, make you whole. *(Acts 9:34)*

I do good and heal all that are oppressed of the devil. *(Acts 10:38)*

My power causes diseases to depart from you. *(Acts 19:12)*

The law of the Spirit of life in Me has made you free from the law of sin and death. *(Romans 8:2)*

The same Spirit that raised Me from the dead now lives in you, and that Spirit will quicken your mortal body. *(Romans 8:11)*

I have made you unto wisdom, righteousness, sanctified, and redeemed. *(1 Corinthians 1:30)*

Your body is a member of Me. *(1 Corinthians 6:15)*

Your body is the temple of My Spirit and you are to glorify Me in your body. *(1 Corinthians 6:19-20)*

If you will rightly discern My body which was broken for you and judge yourself, you will not be judged and you will not be weak, sickly, or die prematurely. *(1 Corinthians 11:29-31)*

I have set gifts of healing in My body. *(1 Corinthians 12:9)*

I have delivered you from death, I do deliver you and, if you will trust Me, I will yet deliver you. *(2 Corinthians 1:10)*

My life may be made manifest in your mortal flesh. *(2 Corinthians 4:10-11)*

I have given you My name and have put all things under your feet. *(Ephesians 1:21-22)*

I want it to be well with you, and I want you to live long on the earth. *(Ephesians 6:3)*

My peace will guard your heart and mind. *(Philippians 4:7)*

I have delivered you from the authority of darkness. *(Colossians 1:13)*

I am faithful. I shall establish you and keep you from evil. *(2 Thessalonians 3:3)*

I will deliver you from every evil work. *(2 Timothy 4:18)*

I tasted death for you. I destroyed the devil who had the power of death. I have delivered you from the fear of death and bondage. *(Hebrews 2:9, 14, 15)*

I wash your body with pure water. *(Hebrews 10:22)*

Lift up the weak hands and the feeble knees. Don't let that which is lame be turned aside, but rather let Me heal it. *(Hebrews 12:12, 13)*

Let the elders anoint you and pray for you in My name and I will raise you up. Pray for one another and I will heal you. *(James 5:14-16)*

By My stripes you were healed. *(1 Peter 2:24)*

My divine power has given unto you all things that pertain unto life and godliness through the knowledge of Me. *(2 Peter 1:3)*

Beloved, I wish above all things that you may be in health. *(3 John 2)*

You overcome Satan by My blood and your testimony. *(Revelation 12:11)*

Whosoever will, let him come and take of the water of life freely. *(Revelation 22:17)*

GOD'S PRESCRIPTION

Take as directed every day to be the fully integrated system God created you to be.

"My son, give attention to my words; incline your ear to my sayings. Do not let them depart from your eyes; keep them in the midst of your heart; for they are life to those who find them, and health to all their flesh. Keep your heart with all diligence, for out of it spring the issues of life. Put away from you a deceitful mouth, and put perverse lips far from you. Let your eyes look straight ahead, and your eyelids look right before you. Ponder the path of your feet, and let all your ways be established. Do not turn to the right or the left; remove your foot from evil."
(Proverbs 4:20-27, NKJV)

I would like to remind you that we are to rely heavily on the grace of God for the healing of our bodies. Sometimes I miss the mark. Does that mean I can't get healed? Absolutely not! I don't get healed on my own merits. I have to rest in the finished work of Christ. It is what He did that heals me, not what I am doing or have done.

These Scriptures are the mark toward which we aim. He keeps my foot from being taken.

"For the LORD shall be thy confidence, and shall keep thy foot from being taken."
(Proverbs 3:26)

"If any of you lacks wisdom, let him ask of God, who gives to all liberally and without reproach, and it will be given to him."
(James 1:5, NKJV)

"It is the Spirit who gives life; the flesh profits nothing. The words that I speak to you are spirit, and they are life."
(John 6:63)

FINAL THOUGHTS

Is what Jesus did enough? Yes! Yes! Yes and Amen! We only need two verses to confirm His victory over Satan and his cohorts.

> *"[God] disarmed the principalities and powers that were ranged against us and made a bold display and public example of them, in triumphing over them in Him and in it [the cross]." (Colossians 2:15, AMP)*

> *"[But] he who commits sin [who practices evildoing] is of the devil [takes his character from the evil one], for the devil has sinned (violated the divine law) from the beginning. The reason the Son of God was made manifest (visible) was to undo (destroy, loosen, and dissolve) the works the devil [has done]." (1 John 3:8, AMP)*

Jesus' work was enough. He finished what He started and completely eradicated what Satan did with Adam. Jesus bought back everything that Adam lost at the fall.

> *"For the sin of this one man, Adam, caused death to rule over many. But even greater is God's wonderful grace and his gift of righteousness, for all who receive it will live in triumph over sin and death through this one man, Jesus Christ." (Romans 5:17, NLT)*

So I say:

Jesus, I cannot thank You enough for all You did for me on Calvary. I worship You and I thank You that I am healed. I lift up the holy name of Jesus and bow my knee to You, my Master and my King. I adore You and magnify Your precious and wonderful blood that was shed for me. Thank You for doing all that You did to save me from the evil one. Thank You for the stripes that were placed upon Your back for my healing. I now take advantage of what You did for me. Thank You!

Hide the Word in your heart. I have spent the last forty-nine years putting the Word of God into my heart. When I had a car wreck and was battling for my life, I didn't even know there was a battle going on because that Word had built a fortress around me, at work in my body, keeping me alive. I could hear the Word of God coming out of my mouth, 'I will bless the Lord at all times, His word will continually be in my mouth' (Psalm 34:1).

I am so grateful that the Lord has kept my family close to Him. Our kids and grandkids all serve the Lord. God has opened many doors for me and has taken me all over this nation and to several foreign countries. He has used me to see many people healed and delivered. God has used my husband many times to teach me about the love of God. I could never have done the things God has allowed me to do if it were not for his love and patience. He has been my constant support and cheerleader. I love this man and I am very thankful for the years of peace I have had in my home.

I decided a long time ago that I would do whatever I learned from the Word. I began to state out loud, 'I am the righteousness of God in Christ and as the righteousness of God I do not have to fight fear.' I spent years building into my spirit being what the Word says. I began to believe the Word more than I believed what the doctors or reports were saying. Even when they had an x-ray hanging on the wall that said I had a mass, I believed the Word. I believed God's Word even when they told me I didn't understand.

I believed the Word of God and what it had to say.

But it was the doctors and nurses that didn't understand. 'I am the righteousness of Christ', and that stuff from the devil, those lying symptoms, cannot stand against the Word of God.

SUMMATION

It is very hard to receive your healing if you don't know for sure that God wants you healed.

F.F. Bosworth said, 'Faith begins where the will of God is known.'

You have to know it is both God's power and His will to save you, and then You will have faith to come and get saved. You also have to know it is God's power and will to heal you. The price has been paid for your healing.

Then you will have the faith to come and be healed.

What Has Been Provided By Grace Must Be Received By Faith

You must receive it with your faith. Just because somebody bought a meal for you does not mean you are going to get full. You have to receive it; appropriate it. EAT!

God is a Good God and Good Things Come From Him

Healing is a good thing. God is my Father and He only wants good things for me. My faith is the key that will open the door to those good things.

> *"Every good gift and every perfect gift is from above, and cometh down from the Father of lights, with whom is no variableness, neither shadow of turning."*
> *(James 1:17)*

Appendix A

PRAYERS FOR HEALING

The following prayers are just guidelines for you to use when you are first starting to pray. Always stay in faith as you pray these prayers and never allow them to become random or just something you memorize. I remind you that these are just examples and not to be thought of as the only way to pray. When I first received Jesus and was first learning how to pray, it would have been a great help to me if I had been given some of these prayers to get me started.

*Thank You, Father, that I can come boldly into Your presence in the name of Your precious Son, Jesus. I thank You, Father, that Jesus bore in His body all my infirmities and all of my iniquities, including the [**name the disease**] that I am experiencing. Since I was healed of this according to 1 Peter 2:24, I therefore seek You for the unique pathway that will lead to a total and complete manifestation of my healing. Through the Holy Spirit, Father, reveal to me all the things that I can do in the natural to overcome this attack and as I do all I can do, Lord, I look to You to do the supernatural that I cannot do. I speak to the [**name the disease**] and I command all systems, organs, muscles, tissues, and cells to return to normal function, in the name of Jesus.*

I thank You, Father, that I have the mind of Christ and that my thoughts will be clear and all symptoms will leave my body. I cast my cares and worries upon You according to 1 Peter 5:7. I call myself healed, and through my eye of faith I see myself healed and believe that the full manifestation of my healing is on the way. I believe, Father, that You will satisfy me with long life and fulfill the number of my days. I thank You that I have authority over the powers of darkness, and in Jesus' name I execute that authority right now and command the grip of darkness to be released from my body. I thank You, Father, that it is done, and as I am set free of all spirits of infirmity and disease, I will find, follow, and complete your divine will for my life. In Jesus' name I pray. Amen.

*Father, in the name of Jesus, I denounce and dig up all the negative words I have spoken against myself. I tell them to dry up and die. I will only say what You say about me. I shall not die but live and declare Your good works. [**Name the disease**] you get out of my body. I pull you up by the roots with the precious blood of Jesus and demand that you leave my body today. I am healed by the stripes of Jesus because He carried my disease for me. Satan, I will not carry your load. I demand that you leave my body now. In Jesus' name. Amen!*

Prayer of Agreement

Find a believer to agree with you about what your need is. Here is a sample of a prayer you can use for agreement.

*[**Name the person**] and I hereby agree according to Matthew 18:19-20, where our Lord Jesus Christ says, 'Again I say unto you . . . if two of you shall agree on earth as touching any thing that they shall ask, it shall be done for them of my Father which is in heaven. For where two or three are gathered together in my name, there am I in the midst of them.' So we agree that this*

*body is healed, this need is met, this bill is paid [**whatever you are agreeing for**], in the name of Jesus. Thank you, Father, for the answer. I believe, I receive.*

You can even sign your names and date it like a legal document. Jesus also said in John 16:23, 'And in that day ye shall ask me nothing. Verily, verily, I say unto you, Whatsoever ye shall ask the Father in my name, he will give it to you.'

Father, in the name of Jesus, we ask:

_____

_____

_____

_____

_____

_____

_____

*Satan, in the name of Jesus, we hereby notify you according to this agreement that you are bound on this day and hour and you will not function, operate, harass, embarrass, or in any way intimidate this agreement because it is done in the name of the Lord Jesus Christ, and we hereby render you helpless in this matter and loose you from your assignment against [**name the person**] and cancel it out, in the name of Jesus.*

In Jesus' name, because we believe and because we know it is so, we set our names to it as a matter of releasing our faith.

Name, Time, and Date _____

Name, Time, and Date _____

Prayers for Specific Ailments

This is not the only way to pray, but it is a way I have found to be effective.

Alzheimer's Disease

I command every legal right of depression invoked by witchcraft oaths to be broken off my life. I come against all ungodly bonding to anyone in my family line with Alzheimer's disease or any other mental or emotional problems. I speak to all emotional or physical withdrawal from my daily life.

I command double mindedness to go. I tell melancholy, mind oppression in my thought processes, any psychotic state, obsessive behavior, mental instability, loss of memory, or anything that has come as a result of family history to get out now. I break every tie to mental confusion and I ask the Lord to bring divine order into my thought processes.

I take full responsibility for any generational sins that might have opened the door to any mental problems. I repent and close the door to any and all mental disorders. I command the curse of Alzheimer's to be broken off my family line and I rebuke any generational curse.

I come against dysfunction of my nervous system and I bind any deterioration of my nervous system. I tell the curse of insanity to get out of my life and the lives of my family. I break any witchcraft oaths that may lead to insanity, dementia, or pronounced senility. I bind emotional insecurity. I praise the Lord for delivering me from any form of mental instability.

I say that my family and I will have a sound mind until the day we go to be with the Lord. In Jesus' name. Amen!

Arthritis

*Father, I come to You in the name of Your precious Son, Jesus, thanking You that Jesus bore in His body two thousand years ago the symptoms of arthritis. I thank You that because He bore this disease in His own body, I was healed! Therefore, I am coming before You to seek the manifestation of that healing in my physical body. In the name of Jesus, I speak to the cartilage in my joints [**name the joints**] and I command that cartilage to increase in thickness and become more pliable and more elastic. I further pray that the inflammatory cells that lead to swelling and pain be removed from that joint. I say, in Jesus' name, that I will be able to move that joint and serve you day by day without pain, symptoms, or inflammation.*

Father, as I do all I can do in the natural, I look to You to do the supernatural that I cannot do. I send forth the healing anointing power of the Holy Spirit, the comforter, who resides within me into my body and into my joints, and I speak comfort and healing to those joints. Thank You, Father, that the manifestation of healing is on the way. I praise You, Father, that You are revealing the specific pathway that I need to walk that leads to my healing. I thank You, Father, for all of these things in the precious name of Jesus, and I close this prayer praising You and thanking You because through my eye of faith, I see myself healed. In Jesus' name. Amen!

Asthma

Father, I come to You in the name of Jesus, praising You as my Healer. I thank You that the manifestation of my healing of asthma is on the way. In accordance to Mark 11:23, I speak specifically to the inflammation edema and inflammatory cells that have been activated in the airways leading to my lungs. I command the sensitivity of these airways to decrease and the inflammation to cease, in the name of Jesus. I say that all symptoms of wheezing, chest tightness, cough, and difficulty breathing will go, in the name of Jesus. Alert and guide me, Father, to those things I can do in the natural to overcome my airway sensitivity. Show me those things to do, Father, to overcome allergies and airborne particles that trigger inflammation in my air passages.

Thank You, Father, for revealing the natural antioxidants, minerals, and fatty acids that will relax the smooth muscle lining of my airways and overcome the inflammation. Instruct and guide me and let Your anointing flow through these substances, Lord, to bring about the manifestation of my healing. Father, alert me as to whether a prescription medicine or inhaler is needed, but I believe that I will be totally delivered and set free from all of the symptoms of asthma. I believe that if Your pathway to healing for me is through prescribed medicines, that I will suffer no harmful or lasting side effects. I am believing You, Lord, to work through natural substances to bring forth my healing.

Thank You, Father, once again, in Jesus' name, that He bore my infirmities in His own body and by His stripes I was healed two thousand years ago. Thank You, Father, that the manifestation of my healing is on the way. In Jesus' name I pray. Amen.

Cancer

Father, I praise You for the authority You have given me over all the power of the enemy that would attack my body. Satan, I bind You with the power of the Holy Spirit, in the name of Jesus. You spirit of cancer, I command you to come out and never return. I speak specifically to my immune system and command the T cells and other components to be activated and to rise up against abnormal cancer cells. I command the cancer's blood supply to wither and die and for the abnormal cell division to stop. I ask You, Father, to reveal to me those natural substances You would have me use to strengthen my immune system. I ask You to reveal those herbal substances and extracts You would have me use to kill and overcome cancer cells in my body. As I do what I can and know to do in the natural, I look to You, Father, to touch my body supernaturally and I thank You that by the stripes of Your Son, Jesus, I was healed and my manifestation of healing is on the way. I thank You for my healing, in Jesus' name. Amen.

Depression

Thank You, Father, that I can come into Your presence in the name of Your Precious Son, Jesus. I thank You, Father, that Jesus bore in His body all my infirmities and all of my iniquities, including the depression that I am experiencing. Since I was healed of this according to 1 Peter 2:24, I now therefore seek You for the unique pathway that will lead to a total and complete manifestation of my healing. Through the Holy Spirit, Father, reveal to me all the things I can do in the natural to overcome this attack, and as I do all I can do, Lord, I look to You to do the supernatural that I cannot do. I speak to the neurotransmitter chemicals in my brain and I command them to be normal, in the name of Jesus. I thank You, Father, that I have the mind of Christ and that my thoughts will be clear and all symptoms of depression will go. I cast my cares and worries upon You according to 1 Peter 5:7 and I call myself healed. Through my eyes of faith, I see myself healed and I believe that the full manifestation of my healing is on the way. I believe, Father, that You will satisfy me with long life and fulfill the number of my days. I thank You that I have authority over the powers of darkness and I execute that power, in Jesus' name, and command the grip of darkness to be released from my mind. Thank You, Father, that it is done, and that I am set free of this depression. I will find, follow and complete Your divine will for my life. In Jesus' name. Amen

Diabetes

Father, in the name of Jesus, I speak to the receptor cells in my body and command them to become more sensitive and less resistant to the effects of insulin, allowing glucose to enter my body cells, supply energy, and perform all the functions You designed. In Jesus' name, I speak to the beta cells of my pancreas and command them to secrete adequate and normal amounts of insulin. I believe, Father, that my blood sugar levels will drop, and my arteries, nerves, and eyes will be protected from destruction caused by high blood sugar levels. Father, I ask You to help me to do my part by maintaining my normal weight and eating proper foods. Father, reveal to me all of the things in the natural that I can do, such as taking supplements, and eating the right foods to take care of this temple. As I do these things in the natural, I will believe and look to You to perform the supernatural in protecting all parts of my body from the effects of diabetes as my insulin levels become normal and my blood sugar levels drop. Thank You, Lord God, that I was healed of this disease by the blood of Jesus two thousand years ago, and I am therefore praying for the full manifestation of healing in my body because by His stripes I was healed. In Jesus' name I pray. Amen.

Energy Increase

Father, I thank You, in Jesus' name, that it is You who gives strength to my body according to Isaiah 40. I claim that strength right now and speak to my energy levels to increase. According to 1 Peter 5:7, I cast upon You all my concerns, worries, and anxieties, which deplete my energy levels. I will wait upon You, Lord, as You renew my strength. I thank You, Father, that You have provided natural substances to further strengthen my physical body. Guide me, Lord, as those substances increase my energy and overcome my fatigue. Let Your anointing flow through my body to increase my strength daily so that I may follow and complete

Your will for my life. I thank You for renewing my physical body and give all the thanks to You, in the name of Jesus. Amen.

Headaches

I come to You, Father, in the name of Jesus, seeking a manifestation of the healing that was purchased for me by Your Son two thousand years ago. Give me wisdom, knowledge, and insight about the headaches I am experiencing, and reveal to me the type of headache and specifically the things that I should do in the natural to overcome this attack. I speak to the muscles in my neck, temple, and scalp area and command them, in the name of Jesus, to relax. I take authority over all of the stress and tension in those muscle groups. Direct me, Father, as to whether I should use natural treatments for these headaches. I further speak to the small arteries in my brain area and command the smooth muscle tone to be normal with no constriction or dilation in these vessels that would cause migraine pain. Direct me, Father, as to the use of natural substances to help with pain and other natural treatments that will maintain the normal tone in these vessels. As I use these natural treatments, Father, I send forth Your anointing into them and command them to work according to Your perfect design. I thank You, Father, that the fear of tumors in my brain, or the fear of going blind, is driven out from my mind and I will walk in divine health. If my doctor recommends a prescription medicine, give me wisdom and insight regarding the use of this medicine as part of my pathway to healing. I thank You, Father, that in Jesus' name I can break the generational and genetic curse of headaches, and I declare that I will be set free of these. Thank You, Father, for all of Your healing provisions and most of all for the name above all names that overcomes the works of the enemy. In Jesus' name, I present these prayers and petitions before You. Amen.

Heart Disease

Father, in the name of Jesus, I thank You for healthy arteries and blood vessels. I know that according to Your Word, that the life of the flesh is in the blood. I therefore speak to the walls and linings of all my arteries according to Mark 11:23. I command any plaque formation to disappear, in the name of Jesus. I further pray, in the name of Jesus, that there will be no clot formation that would obstruct the blood vessels. I pray specifically that the platelets in my bloodstream will function normally and in a manner that will not cause a clot to block the normal flow of blood. I thank You, Father, for revelation knowledge of the things I can do in the natural to reverse any cholesterol plaque that has formed and prevent any plaque from forming in the future. Reveal to me, Lord, those specific vitamins, minerals, supplements, herbs, and whatever other natural sources I should be using to protect my blood vessels and vital organs and reverse any damage that has already occurred. I thank You, Father, that my coronary arteries will supply blood to my heart muscle as You designed them to do. I pray that my carotid arteries and all of the cerebral arteries supplying blood to my brain will remain free of blockage and free of blood clots. Thank You that my kidneys will function normally and the circulation throughout all of my extremities will be normal. I thank You, Father, that Your Son, Jesus, bore in His own body on the cross all artery problems that I might ever face and by His stripes I was healed two thousand years ago. I will endeavor to do all that I can and all that I know to do to protect my arteries and my vascular system. I will trust You, Father, to do the supernatural that I cannot do as my greatest and fondest desire is to finish the course to which You have called me and to finish it with joy. In Jesus' name I pray. Amen.

*Important note on Heart Disease

There are many factors that interact to cause heart disease and hardening of the arteries, but the most common and most basic underlying problem is the formation of a cholesterol plaque on the artery walls that causes a disruption in the normal blood flow. In order to pray with understanding we have to be able to speak to these specific processes such as plaque formation, cholesterol deposits, and blood clot formation. The more specifically we speak to the mountain and take authority over it, the more effective our prayer. It would be wise for all of us to speak to our arteries and bind the formation of blood clots, whether we have been diagnosed with heart disease or not.

Hypoglycemia

Father, in the name of Jesus, I thank You that my pancreas is functioning normally. I thank You that my blood sugar levels will not drop too low, and as I consume increased amounts of fiber in my diet, the natural sugar that I do consume will be absorbed slowly and evenly, causing my insulin levels to change within a normal range. I stand against all symptoms of fatigue, tiredness, dizziness, light-headedness, and drops in blood pressure that may be caused by rapid drops in my blood sugar or low blood sugar. As I do things in the natural, nutritionally, to guard the secretion of insulin in my body, I thank You that You will supernaturally regulate the beta cells of my pancreas to produce normal amounts of insulin and that I will not experience any symptoms associated with low blood sugar. Thank You, Father, for guarding and protecting this temple and giving me Your wisdom of my body's wonderful design. In Jesus' name I pray. Amen.

Immune System

Father, I thank You for Your hand of protection that rests over me. I thank You also for the natural protection You created in my body through my immune system. I therefore speak specifically to the lymphocytes and command them in Jesus' name to become activated and balanced. I speak to the T cells, the B cells, the macrophage cells, and the natural killer cells and command them to function strongly and in the balance that You created them. I thank You, Father, that as I supplement my temple with various natural substances, that Your anointing will flow through these natural substances to strengthen and balance my immune system.

Thank You that my immune system will instantly recognize and overcome any foreign invader or any process that occurs in my body that does not line up with Your Word. I further thank You, Lord, that my immune system will maintain the proper balance and not become over-activated as a result of fighting off foreign invaders and substances. I will walk in Your divine protection, Father, doing all I can do in the natural to enhance this incredible immune system. I will trust You to provide the supernatural protection that I cannot. I thank You for all of these things, Father, and I give You all of the glory. In the precious name of Jesus. Amen.

Leg Cramps

Father, I come before You in the mighty name of Jesus, thanking You for strong and normally functioning extremities. I thank You, Father, that the sensory nerves of my lower extremities will function normally and the abnormal sensations I have experienced will cease, in the name of Jesus. I thank You, Father, that the motor nerves that go to the muscles in my legs will be normal and I command the restlessness and movement of the legs to cease, in Jesus' name. Thank You, Lord, that I will be satisfied with peaceful, restful sleep as I come against the torment of leg cramps and restless legs.

Father, I thank You that You have provided a pathway of healing for me through natural substances. Direct me, Lord, to the natural supplements You would have me use and let Your anointing flow through these to bring healing to my legs. Through my eye of faith, I am healed, and I give You praise and glory for revealing the schemes and devices of the enemy that have come against me.

Thank You, Lord, that greater is He that is in me than he that is in the world. In Jesus' name, I thank You for this healing. Amen.

Multiple Sclerosis

Father, I come to You in the name of Jesus, thanking You for the healing that Your Son, Jesus, bore for me in His own body. In His name, I speak to the lining of my nerves. I command the inflammation to cease, and my immune system to reverse its attack upon my nerve system.

I say, in the name of Jesus, that the myelin sheaths that have been destroyed will be restored. I say there will be no further damage to the myelin sheaths of my nerves and that all symptoms in my body will go into permanent remission and I will be healed.

I thank You, Father, for the wisdom and knowledge as to how I can receive the proper balance of food substances, such as fatty acids in my body, to overcome the inflammation. I thank You for the antioxidants that will further diminish the inflammation and for the vitamins that will restore normal nerve conduction throughout my body.

Let Your anointing flow through these substances. In Jesus' name, I speak restoration to my nerves and my immune system. As I do these things that You have revealed to me in the natural, I look to You, Father, to perform the supernatural restoration in my nervous system. I thank You, Father, that I was healed, and therefore I am healed in Jesus' name. I give You all the praise and glory for the full manifestation of my healing from multiple sclerosis. Amen.

Muscular System

- Command voluntary muscles (skeletal muscles) to relax.
- Command tightness and rigidity out and tendons (connecting tissue) to relax.

- Call out cramps, spasms, and pain.
- Call out any muscle deterioration.
- Command healing to the discs in the back and call them into the right position.
- Command muscles, ligaments, tendons, and nerves to be healed.
- Command the tail bone to move into proper position.
- Command circulation to be restored and blood vessels cleared of any foreign material build up, and swelling to go.
- Command ligaments to line up with the Word.

Organs, Systems, and Glands

I speak to every organ in my body and command all of them to operate and function at 100% efficiency the way God made them to do so. My heart is strong and healthy, with every valve working in perfect harmony. My heart beats in perfect rhythm. All the blood vessels surrounding my heart are free from blockages of any kind. My liver, kidneys, and lungs all operate and function effectively and efficiently, with no hindrances. All my organs function and perform their duties effectively. All my organs are healthy and whole. They are free from sickness, disease, growths, and tumors.

Every system in my body operates like a well-oiled machine. My nervous system, my electrical system, my circulatory system, my lymphatic system, my digestive system, my endocrine system, and every other system in my body operate in total and complete harmony with each other. My systems are free from sickness, disease, growths, or tumors of any kind.

I speak life and health to all the glands in my body and proclaim that they are healthy and whole. My adrenal glands, thyroid gland, pituitary gland, and all other glands in my body operate and function at 100% efficiency. They are free from all sickness, disease, growths, and tumors. My body is healed, healthy, and whole. I am full of vim, vigor, and vitality. Thank you, my precious Jesus!

Restoration

I thank You, Father, that You said You would make up for the years of great devastation that the enemy has brought on me. You said You would restore the years the deadly locust, the savage locusts, and the locust of doom have eaten.

I thank You, right now, that the enemy has to bring back what he has stolen from me. Proverbs says that when a thief is caught he has to pay back seven times what he has stolen. So bring back to me every dime I have been cheated out of, every penny that belongs to me that I never received, bring it back, Lord! I speak to all that was lost and say, 'Come back to me now, in Jesus' name!'

Bring back to me the funds taken from my ancestors who never had the revelation of what they had sown. Restore to our family all the money stolen, all the time stolen, all the peace, and all the relationships that have been ruined. Bring back marriages, families, and relationships. Satan, you get your hands off whatever concerns us, in Jesus' name. Restore to us, Father, health, mind function, abilities, and anything else Satan has stolen from us. Restore our youth. Father, we come against old age spirits coming on us before our time. We reclaim mind and body functions that have been taken from us. We repent for the misuse of our bodies and declare that they begin to function properly. We bind the spirits of diabetes, cancer, arthritis, dementia, cerebral palsy, and any other disease that tries to come on our bodies.

Give it all back! May we begin to reap from those whom we have helped. We claim the funds from those who went home to be with Jesus before seeing their harvest for the Kingdom of God. Give it up, devil, it is payback time. Bring back what you stole! Satan, you bring it all back!

Father, You said in Joel that I will eat my fill of good food, I will be full of praises to You, and that I will never again be despised. So, we thank You for enforcing what You promised in Your Word. Thank You for the financial and physical blessings that we are about to receive.

Skin Disease

Father, I thank You, in the name of Jesus, for healthy skin. I thank You, Father, for the revelation of natural substances from Your plant and animal kingdom that You have provided for me to protect my skin. I thank You that my skin will secrete the proper amounts of oil to keep the skin surface lubricated. I thank You, Father, for the supplements You have provided to support my underlying skin structure. I pray for wisdom and direction in utilizing supplements to my diet to reverse age-related changes and maintain healthy skin. Thank You, Father, that abnormal cell divisions in my skin that would result in skin cancers will not occur. I thank You for the natural substances I can use to protect myself from skin cancers. Thank You, Father, that as I utilize these various substances and do what I can do in the natural, You will place Your supernatural hand of protection upon my body. I thank You that right now, as I lay my hands upon my body, that if there are any abnormal cells, they will wither and die. My confession is that no skin malignancy will exist in this temple. Thank You, Father, for Your divine protection and provision in this vital area of my body. In Jesus' name I pray. Amen.

Supernatural Strength

Father, I thank You that I am strong in the Lord and in the power of His might. The joy of the Lord is my strength, and His strength sustains me. I am full of energy; I am vibrant and full of life and vitality. God in me is stronger than any weakness in my flesh. It doesn't matter how I feel because I am not moved by feelings. I speak supernatural strength, energy, and vitality in my body. Weakness, tiredness, and weariness, I command you to get out of my body now, in the name of Jesus.

I can do all things through Christ who strengthens me. I have dynamic energy and indomitable strength. I am undaunted in my faith. I am strong in the Lord. I am courageous and fearless. Greater is He that is in me than he that is in the world. His strength rises up in me. He puts me above my feelings. I am strong in my spirit. I am strong in my mind. I am strong in my body. My strength is renewed like the eagles. God increases my strength; therefore, I am not weary. I thank You, Father, in Jesus' name. Amen!

As a side note, I want to stress that these prayers for specific diseases are not meant to be a diagnosis for healing. They are here to help you pray as specifically as you can. I am not a doctor and am in no way trying to diagnose your symptoms. This is written to assist you with scriptures to pray.

Victory Over Death

The fear of death has no sting for me! Death, I have no fear of you! Jesus tasted death for me. I have life, His life, in me. Now, fear, you will bow your knee!

I cast you out, now, in the name of Jesus who lives in me, loves me, and will love me and stay with me forever.

I thank You, Jesus, for Your promises. I am blessed!

Condemnation has no place in my life. I cast you out in the name of Jesus.

Jesus is my Savior, Redeemer, lover of my soul, Bread of Life, Living Word, the One whom I love and serve forever. There is no condemnation against me, because I am in Christ Jesus. You see I do not walk after the flesh, I walk after the Spirit.

I declare that the law of the Spirit of life in Christ Jesus has set me free from the law of sin and death. (Romans 8:2)

MY PERSONAL HEALING PRAYERS

Appendix B

TESTIMONIES

From the time I accepted Jesus, God began to use me for the miraculous. I have seen dozens of instant miracles when I have laid my hands on people. God has used me to lay hands on people who have experienced creative miracles more than once.

My daughter-in-law had one of her kidneys removed when she was eight years old. She had been in pain all of her life from a rare disease that had eaten most of that kidney. After the surgery, she appeared to be fine until she and my son were married. She began to have pain again and lots of kidney infections. The doctors were concerned that the disease had returned and was in her other kidney. They scheduled her to have dye run into the kidney so that they could see what was going on. The Lord spoke to me one morning after our family had prayed together the night before. I had read a book about a young man who had gone to heaven in a dream. He said there was a room there filled with body parts and had asked what they were for. He was told that they were for God's people. The angel told him that the reason people didn't have the parts was that no one on the earth had been willing to do the warfare necessary to get the parts past the heavens where Satan, the god of this world battles. I told the Lord I would do the warfare and I charged the angel, the one the Bible says we have (Hebrews 1:14), to go and get Char a kidney from the room holding the body parts. I told the angel that I would do the warfare to get him and the kidney through. All day long I seemed to sense when the angel needed me to intercede. I prayed and did warfare all day. That night I called my daughter-in-law and told her what the Lord had shown me. She said, 'Oh, Mom, I receive that.' When they did the test and ran the dye through her kidney, thinking they would only find one kidney, they found two perfect kidneys. She has had no more infections. That was over twenty years ago. They had also told her she would probably never have children because of the scar tissue but she has three beautiful, healthy children.

I prayed for a young man named CJ with cerebral palsy who could not walk. He was in a wheelchair and someone brought him up to the second floor where I was praying. When he came, he could hardly talk, he had food all over himself, and his head and arms moved uncontrollably. I asked what he wanted from God, and he managed to tell me that he wanted to walk. We prayed for him and got him up out of the wheelchair. We walked him for twenty minutes and sat him down in a regular chair. Two weeks later when I met him at church, he was walking with canes and talking normally. He was clean and his hair was combed. He has been healthy ever since.

I prayed for a five-year-old little boy named Jimmy whose eyes were crossed. He was scheduled for surgery at the end of the week. I sat him on my lap and told him, 'Jimmy, Jesus is going to heal your eyes.' The next morning when he got up, his eyes were straight and have been so ever since.

I prayed for an eleven-year-old young girl who was born with a leg that was a foot shorter than the other and her hands and arms faced backwards and bent toward her wrists. When I prayed, God grew her leg out and she was able to run and skip for the first time in her life. He also turned her hands and arms forward.

I prayed for a five-year-old girl named Cassie who accidentally drank gasoline when she was eighteen months old and could not speak properly. When she tried to talk, she just made sounds that didn't make sense. She was a very hyper child and when I picked her up she went lifeless in my arms. I prayed for her and handed her back to her dad. She was out cold. (I think they thought I had killed her.) From the time she woke up until now, she has spoken normally.

I spoke at a Women's Aglow years ago in Freeport, IL. There was a lady there who needed a new heart. They carried her up to me, I prayed for her and she slumped to the floor. We called for her to have a new heart. I received a call from her family about a week later telling me she had been to the doctor and he told her she had a brand new heart. I have seen her since and she is running five miles a day and looks great.

I went to Beulah, ND, years ago to do a Healing Revival. There was a lady who came who was born without a hip socket. My friend, who had gone with me, and I laid our hands on her. She grew a hip socket. She could stand straight for the first time in her life.

I prayed for a lady who had brain cancer. She had come for radiation treatments at Swedish American Hospital's Cancer Treatment Center. She told me this was her last treatment because they had told her they couldn't do anything else. They were sending her home to die. She told me she had three little kids, she was in her early thirties and she lived on Brooke Road in Rockford, IL. I prayed with her to accept Jesus and laid hands on her before her treatment. I received a phone call from someone I knew about ten years later. She asked me if I had ever prayed with a lady who was in her early thirties, had three little kids, and lived on Brooke Road who had brain cancer. I told her I had. She began to yell, 'I knew it, I knew it! She said it was a red-headed lady who prayed for her at Swede's Oncology Department and she got healed.'

I prayed for a lady who was dying with cirrhosis of the liver. They had given her days to live. I laid my hands on her and she was healed completely.

I prayed for a man named Donnie who suffered with a herniated disc in his back. He was to have surgery the next day. I anointed him with oil and showed him in the Scriptures what it said belonged to him as a believer and he was instantly healed. They did intensive tests on him and could find nothing to operate on.

I mentioned earlier that I had a car wreck several years ago and I crushed my shoulder, broke four ribs, had internal bleeding, and a punctured lung. God did some instant miracles and they transferred me to another hospital. I still had four broken ribs and a broken scapula. The doctor told me that he should have operated, but that there was not much to pin to, and that it was not my primary arm. He said it was a hard operation and that I would just have to learn to live with it. He said that my shoulder would be like an arthritic shoulder with pain when the weather changed. He told me that I would have limited use of the arm. I told him that I could take the Word of God and change that. I began to speak to my shoulder. I told it what the Word said about the situation: 'You are quickened and made alive according to Romans 8:11.' In six weeks that bone in my shoulder had grown together and I have had no pain since.

My son had ingrown toenails so bad that they bled every day. The doctor wanted to operate on them, but we spoke to those toes for one year. We told the toes what God said about their healing and today he has the nicest toes you have ever seen.

My other son fell and broke both elbows and both wrists. They were going to operate, but we prayed and all they did was set the wrists and elbows. In one week one elbow was out of the cast and the next week they removed the other one. When they did the x-rays, they couldn't see that they were ever broken. That same son broke his knee once; we prayed and it was healed instantly. He was also healed of asthma.

My daughter had tumors in her nose. We scheduled her for surgery. I took her to church and had an old man in the prayer room anoint her with oil. All the tumors disappeared and the surgery was cancelled.

My husband and I went to visit his sister in Arkansas several years ago. She had a nine-month-old baby who was the sickest little baby

I had ever seen. She couldn't even cry, all she did was make sounds. She had to drink goat's milk and was allergic to everything. They had run tests on her the week before and had sent her home for the weekend. The doctors said they were not sure what the problem was. The parents were to take her back to the hospital on Monday. I explained to the mother how Jesus had redeemed us from the curse of the law, and that if she would believe the baby had been redeemed from this illness, I would anoint her with oil and the baby would be healed. She began to cry and said she had never heard that before. I anointed the baby with oil and we prayed the prayer of faith. The baby instantly got better. She quit making sounds and began to be hungry. When they took her back to the hospital on Monday, the doctors said she had spinal-meningitis; very contagious and very dangerous. My sister-in-law convinced the doctor to redo the tests and they found that she was perfectly whole. She never had any more symptoms. She is now a gynecologist. She and her husband helped start a church in one of the Caribbean islands a few years ago.

My husband's sister who got hold of faith when her baby was sick, just had several massive strokes only weeks ago and was paralyzed on one side and in a coma. Her brain was bleeding and they were going to operate on her the next morning. The family called us to pray and the next morning she woke up perfectly normal. No bleeding and full usage of her body. The doctors recognized that she had a miracle. She went home quickly. She found out that the same faith in the Word of God that healed her daughter would also work for her.

I could go on for hours about the legs I have seen grow out, the backs that have been healed, and the people who have been told they were dying. But when my prayer buddy, Bev Tucker, and I would pray, they would receive their healing and go home. I have prayed for deformed arms that were healed, feet turned inward that have been healed, and two cases where people that wore platform shoes due to physical issues had to go home without shoes because they had received their healing and their legs were even.

One of these was a young lady in her teens in Poland who came to the meeting with these shoes because one of her legs was shorter than the other. After prayer, she left barefoot because her platform shoe caused the other leg to be too short.

The other was an older gentleman in his nineties who had one leg six inches shorter than the other and had worn a platform shoe since he was in his twenties. His leg grew out and they had to buy him a new pair of shoes.

God has been so tremendous to allow me to be a part of so many miraculous things. I cannot thank Him enough.

I can only trust that these testimonies will inspire you to pursue the healing you need.

I am quick to add that in no way am I saying, 'Look what I have done.' Jesus is the only hero of my story. I will be eternally grateful that He has used me to be a part of what He is doing on this earth. He has graced me with an anointing that has allowed me to lay hands on thousands of people and see them healed. For that, I give Him praise. He has blessed me with the opportunity to lead hundreds and hundreds of people to the Lord, and see many baptized in the Holy Spirit. I am so honored to be a small part of His plan.

MY TESTIMONY OF HEALING

Appendix C

GENERAL INFORMATION

Following is some information that I have gathered through research (Internet, etc.) about various diseases and conditions, *but it is not meant to be used to provide a diagnosis or a cure.* Please do your own research regarding the disease you are battling!

Cardiovascular Disease—Mitral Valve Prolapse

Cardiovascular disease can be broken into three classes involving three different spiritual roots. The first class includes angina and arrhythmias, caused by fear, anxiety, and stress. 'In the last days, men's hearts shall fail them because of fear' (Luke 21:26).

All of these arrhythmic problems are the result of fear, anxiety, and stress because the first receptor cell of fear through the hypothalamus is the heart muscle. Just as the nerve signal is interrupted in the mitral valve prolapse, so it is interrupted in heart arrhythmias. Suppressed stress and anger can reduce white blood cells, as in the case of mitral valve prolapse. For a long time, we were told that mitral valve prolapse was the result of an infection, but for several years now we have known that it is an anxiety disorder. It results from a neurological imbalance coming out of the mind-body connection.

When you are not at peace with God, yourself, and others, your body will respond neurologically. There is an interruption of the nerve transmission controlling the mitral valve, which regulates the flow of blood through the heart. Mitral valve prolapse is now considered a syndrome. It is associated with a slight imbalance in the autonomic nervous system. The autonomic or unconscious nervous system controls and affects most, if not all, of our body functions and systems. This includes our heart rate, blood pressure, body temperature, sweating, gastrointestinal motility and secretions, digestion, and sexual responses, just to name a few.

Stressful stimuli such as fear, rage, anger, or even job pressure can elicit a stress response from our autonomic nervous system causing the valve to malfunction and not open and close properly. Mitral valve prolapse is a common cardiac condition that is thought to affect 10% to 20% of the general population. Both males and females are affected. Females outnumber males by 3 to 1. It is hereditary, but not from a genetic standpoint. Recent studies have shown that approximately 40% to 60% of symptomatic mitral valve prolapse patients also suffer from panic attacks.

Cancer—Fact or Truth

"He rescued me from my powerful enemy, from my foes, who were too strong for me. They confronted me in the day of my disaster, but the LORD was my support."
(Psalm 18:17-18, NIV)

"He rescued me from my powerful enemies, from those who hated me and were too strong for me. They attacked me at a moment when I was in distress, but the LORD supported me."
(Psalm 18:17-18, NLT)

When the doctor says you have cancer, your normal reaction is one of fear. YOU MUST RESIST THAT! It is normal to feel fear at that time but you must not let it enter your heart. Be very careful what you say about yourself. Do not come into agreement with the diagnosis. Do not deny its presence, but you can deny its legal right to be there. When your mind hears the word 'cancer', it will send a message to your body: shut down. Come against that immediately. Rebuke 'shut down' in the name of Jesus. Begin to say, 'By the stripes of Jesus I am healed and made whole.'

Remember, God is not cursing you because of some past sin. Don't believe any of the devil's lies. **You are in covenant with Almighty God and you are the righteousness of God in Christ and, as such, cancer does not have a legal right to live in you.**

The doctors use what is called Overall Stage Grouping to describe the progression of cancer: 0 through 5. Stage 0 is cancer that involves only the cells in which it began and has not spread to other tissues.

Prayer

*I ask You, Father, by the cleansing blood of Jesus Christ, to purify my blood cells and drive out every cancerous cell forming in my body and bring total healing in the area [**be very specific where it is trying to operate**], in Jesus' name. I receive healing now in Jesus' name.*

*My body is the temple of God. I ask You, Father, to stop cancer from moving into other areas of my body and bring total healing in the area [**name the area**], in Jesus' name. I declare the Word of God to be true and receive my complete healing. I enforce the Word that declares that You will perfect that which concerns me. I tell my body what to do, 'You are healed, act like it.'*

Cancer has the ability to not only travel through the veins, but can create its own path through the body.

Prayer

Father, I refuse to give a legal right of way to every path in my body that has cancer traveling through it. I will not give you the right of passage. I ask for Your grace and healing in this part of my body. Thank You, Father, that as I enforce what You said in Your Word, You back Your Word. It will not return void or non-productive.

Stage 2 cancers are locally advanced, cancer that has spread from where it started to nearby tissue or lymph nodes. Lymph nodes filter the lymphatic fluid and store special cells that can trap cancer cells or bacteria that are traveling through the body in the lymph fluid. The lymph nodes are critical for the body's immune response and are principal sites where many immune reactions are initiated. During a physical examination doctors often look for swollen lymph nodes in areas where lymph nodes are abundant, including the neck, around the collarbone, the armpit, and the groin.

No matter whether it is a stage 2, 3, or 4 type of cancer, 'Is anything too hard for God?' *I shall live and not die and declare the works of the Lord* (Psalm 118:17).

Fear always tries to come with a serious diagnosis. The devil will try to make you fearful and anxious. If he can keep you ignorant of what belongs to you, he can kill you. Fear, anxiety, and depression may have the ability to stop your healing. You may fear you have a lack of faith and that is why you have cancer in the first place.

God said in His Word that He has given each man the measure of faith.

> *"For I say, through the grace given unto me, to every man*
> *that is among you, not to think of himself more highly than*
> *he ought to think; but to think soberly, according as God hath*
> *dealt to every man the measure of faith."*
> *(Romans 12:3)*

Satan may try to tell you that you must have missed God and this is the result. You must be doing something wrong. *You may just have done something right!*

The curse is out there and somehow the enemy has laid this on you. This does not mean you have to take it. RESIST THESE SYMPTOMS. If you think you have missed it, repent and move on.

God has not given you a spirit of fear, but one of power, love, and of a sound mind. Romans 8:14 says, 'For as many as are led by the Spirit of God, they are the sons of God.' As a son or daughter of God, you have certain rights that the devil hopes you don't know about. You must know what belongs to you.

Check your heart and see if you have anything hidden, or something you need to confess. If you find something there, just confess it!

"So now there is no condemnation for those who belong to Christ Jesus. And because you belong to him, the power of the life-giving Spirit has freed you from the power of sin that leads to death."
(Romans 8:1-2, NLT)

MAKE SURE YOU KNOW THE TRUTH!

What to do now

One of the hardest things for people who have received a bad report is deciding what to do about treatments.

"If you need wisdom, ask our generous God, and he will give it to you. He will not rebuke you for asking."
(James 1:5, NLT)

"A cheerful heart is good medicine, but a broken spirit saps a person's strength."
(Proverbs 17:22, NLT)

Ask the Lord what you should do concerning your pathway to healing. He may send you to a special doctor, or He may tell you to stand on the Word. Listen carefully to that still small voice and follow it to the letter.

"You will keep in perfect peace all who trust in you, all whose thoughts are fixed on you!"
(Isaiah 26:3, NLT)

No matter what the treatment, do not be moved by the cancer markers or other test results. This is a mistake; put your trust in the covenant you have with God.

Make the Word of God more real to you than your symptoms are. You do that by meditating on the Word daily.

Meditate on the Word of God, especially the healing scriptures. Make them your own. You do that by keeping them in the forefront of your mind and heart. Confess them every time you think of it.

"Study this Book of Instruction continually. Meditate on it day and night so you will be sure to obey everything written in it. Only then will you prosper and succeed in all you do."
(Joshua 1:8, NLT)

I WOULD HIGHLY RECOMMEND THAT YOU KEEP PEOPLE AWAY FROM YOU WHO HAVE A NEGATIVE ATTITUDE. You do not need anyone telling you how to die. You need people who will encourage you with the Word of God. Don't listen to people who want to tell you about dear ones who 'believed God and died anyway'. They will only discourage you. God wants you to live and live life abundantly.

Be careful where you allow your mind to wander.

"I will not die; instead, I will live to tell what the LORD has done."
(Psalm 118:17, NLT)

Remember that faith works by love, and love covers a multitude of sins.

"I prayed to the LORD, and he answered me. He freed me from all my fears. In my desperation I prayed, and the LORD listened; he saved me from all my troubles. Even strong young

lions sometimes go hungry, but those who trust in the LORD *will lack no good thing. The* LORD *hears his people when they call to him for help. He rescues them from all their troubles. The* LORD *is close to the brokenhearted; he rescues those whose spirits are crushed. The righteous person faces many troubles, but the* LORD *comes to the rescue each time."*
(Psalm 34:4, 6, 10, 17-19)

"Beloved, I pray that you may prosper in all things and be in health, just as your soul prospers."
(3 John 2, NKJV)

"The thief's purpose is to steal and kill and destroy. My purpose is to give them a rich and satisfying life."
(John 10:10, NLT)

"I am come that they might have life, and that they might have it more abundantly."
(John 10:10, KJV)

*I wish to insert a word of caution here. We are to be wise in our eating, but God told us that our food is to be sanctified by prayer and the Word of God.

"Forbidding to marry, and commanding to abstain from meats, which God hath created to be received with thanksgiving of them which believe and know the truth. For every creature of God is good, and nothing to be refused, if it be received with thanksgiving: For it is sanctified by the word of God and prayer."
(1 Timothy 4:3-5)

Pray over what you eat and believe God to cleanse it for your body's use. Don't put your trust in a diet or supplements. Don't even put your faith in anything other than God's Word and what He says about your healing. Remember, people say a Mediterranean diet is best but the people in Jesus' day only ate a Mediterranean diet and yet they came to Him sick and in need of healing. It is good to follow a certain diet, take supplements, exercise, drink plenty of water, and get plenty of rest, but don't place your faith in any of these. Your faith should be planted deeply in 'By His stripes you are healed!'

Place your faith firmly in the Word of God and what God says about your healing. Listen to Him! He may tell you to drink more water, get more sleep, stop doing something, or start doing something. Whatever He says to you, do it! Begin to thank Him for your healing and keep your trust planted in Him. He loves you and wants you healed.

A Word of Caution

Forgiveness and bitterness put the body into a stressful environment. Learn to have a loving and forgiving spirit. Learn to relax and enjoy life.

> *"Don't worry about anything; instead, pray about everything. Tell God what you need, and thank him for all he has done."* *(Philippians 4:6, NLT)*

Again I tell you . . . do not put your faith in a diet, a doctor, a method, or your eating habits. Put your faith ONLY IN THE GREAT PHYSICIAN, JESUS CHRIST. PUT YOUR TRUST IN HIM ALONE TO HEAL YOUR BODY.

WHY DO I BELIEVE SO STRONGLY?

I will try and explain to you a little about how God called me and changed me.

I came out of a broken home, raised by my mom and grandmother until the age of five when my mother remarried. My dad had run away and left us when I was two. My mother was left with me and another baby on the way. The Red Cross searched and found that my dad had joined the Army. He told the Army that he was single and sent his allotment check to his mother. When he came out of the Army, he convinced my mother to agree to a divorce. My mother was a believer and didn't believe in divorce.

He proceeded to go from woman to woman. The fact is that I have two half-sisters that I don't even know. I don't even know their last names or if they are still alive.

I grew up angry and rebellious. I had a very good stepfather but I always felt left out of everything. I never felt that I belonged or that I was good enough to be loved.

I married at eighteen and had two children who are my treasures. At twenty-five I was divorced, which left me even angrier and more rebellious. I loved my kids and was determined to raise them in a peaceful home.

I married my present husband, Roy, at the age of twenty-six. We were married in April of 1967, and gave our hearts to the Lord together in November of the same year in a Baptist church.

We were led to an Assemblies of God church where we served for thirty years.

We stayed in church, serving the Lord and loving Him with all our hearts. We were determined to be all that the Lord wanted us to be.

Ten years ago God led us to Life Church in Roscoe, IL. A few years later I received my pastoral license and later was ordained. Pastor Kevin Kringel, senior leader of Life Church, put me on staff a short time later, and that is my position today.

I was an angry, rebellious woman who was scared of everything, BUT God proceeded to deliver me from fear and began to work on my temperament. People always said I had a temper because of the red hair, but I knew it was a whole lot more than that.

It took years of taking the Word of God and letting Him work anger and rebellion out of me. I kept saying about me what God had to say about me.

I was terribly afraid of thunderstorms. I would take my Bible and sit at the bottom of the basement steps rocking my Bible. I thought the next clap of thunder was going to kill me. Everybody knows thunder won't hurt you, but that kind of fear is not rational.

At the present time I am no longer afraid of storms. Knowing what the Word says about my safety, when a tornado is approaching my vicinity, I go out and talk to it. I tell it not to come near me or my loved ones, in the name of Jesus. Jesus spoke to storms and said I would do the things He did. So without fear, I tell it to pass over us. I now know who I am and what belongs to me. I also know the authority I have through what is said in the Word of God. I just tell the storms what He said to them, 'Peace be still!'

That is what the Lord Jesus is able to do for a person who wholly gives themselves to Him. He will turn you into a different person: a person that loves God and loves people.

God allowed me to lead my dad to the Lord three weeks before he died. ONLY GOD CAN DO SUCH MIRACLES!

Only He can take a young, rebellious, angry, full-of-fear person who didn't trust anyone, and turn her into a lady who loves and trusts God and loves people. I was also able to lead my ex-husband to the Lord and my present husband's ex-wife in the prayer of salvation before they passed from this life. Only God!

After receiving the Holy Spirit, with the evidence of speaking in tongues, I began praying for people to be healed and started to see their healings manifest. People began to call me to come pray for them. God began to open doors for me to minister to all kinds of people. I will always be grateful to Him for all He has done for me, and my family.

God taught me early how to break soul ties and generational curses off my children. We have had no divorces or rebellious children, for which I am so very thankful.

I have always tried to go where I am called, so in a very real sense this book is my way of going where I cannot physically go.

God has sent me all over this nation and to several foreign countries to bring people to Jesus and see them healed and delivered. I have laid my hands on thousands of people and have seen them healed. God has allowed me to lead thousands of people to the saving knowledge of Jesus Christ. I also have prayed for many, many, many people to be filled with the Holy Spirit with the evidence of speaking in tongues. All the praise goes to Jesus for His wonderful grace and mercy in allowing me to be used in this fashion. He has given me the opportunity of ministering to the elderly, the middle aged, and the young—even babies. He has allowed me to speak into the lives of people of all ages, colors, and backgrounds. To Him be all the glory. I can never thank Him enough.

Please understand that in no way do I want to portray to you that I think I have all the answers. I can only say that I have learned a few things that have worked for me, and I have backed my information with scriptures. If I can help you realize some of these wonderful truths as well, then it is worth putting down on paper. You can take my suggestions in this book and work them out with prayer and meditation of the Word into your own situation.

If I have repeated myself, please forgive me. I have endeavored to show you what God can do with a life totally submitted to Him. He can take a badly broken life and change it into a life that He can use in the Kingdom of God. Jesus has been a constant Guide and Friend to me and has kept me healthy and sound. He is not finished with me yet, praise His holy name.

Thank you so much and may God bless you,
Evelyn Gipson

ABOUT THE AUTHOR

Pastor Evelyn Gipson is a ministry co-worker at Life Church Assembly of God in Roscoe, Illinois under the apostolic covering of the Assemblies of God Presbyter and Lead Pastor Kevin Kringel.

She is co-pastor of the Abundant Living Discipleship Classes at Life Church and has worked alongside Pastor Beverly Tucker for ten years. Their longtime friendship has brought the development of a strong love for the Lord, a love for people, and a passion to see the body of Christ come into agreement with healing for the body, the mind, and the soul.

Evelyn is known for her strong gift of faith. Those working with her have witnessed her hard work and dedication first hand as she continues to develop in the ways of God and deepens her relationship with the Lord. God has blessed her with a healing anointing that He uses to touch people in pain. She has been diligent throughout her ministry career to study the life of Jesus, His ministry, His teachings, and all that the blood of Jesus does for the body of Christ.

Evelyn's tremendous love for people has launched her into this evangelistic call on her life. Evangelism remains a huge part of her ministry and is the main focus for the establishment of the healing ministry to which God has called her. She always has a testimony and not many get by her without hearing something about what God has done or is doing. If you see her out and about, you can be sure she will be bragging on God and marking people for His kingdom.

Evelyn and Roy, her husband of forty-nine years, make their home in Machesney Park, Illinois. They have five children and ten grandchildren.

PRAYER

We hope you enjoyed this book and that it has been both a blessing and a challenge to your life and walk with God. Maybe you just got hold of it and are looking through before starting. We made the decision as a publishing company to never take for granted that everyone has prayed a prayer to receive Jesus as their Lord, so we include that as the finale to this book. If you have never asked Jesus into your life and would like to do that now, it's so easy. Just pray this simple prayer:

Dear Lord Jesus, thank You for dying on the cross for me. I believe that You gave Your life so that I could have life. When You died on the cross, You died as an innocent man who had done nothing wrong. You were paying for my sins and the debt I could never pay. I believe in You, Jesus, and receive the brand new life and fresh start that the Bible promises that I can have. Thank You for my sins forgiven, for the righteousness that comes to me as a gift from You, for hope and love beyond what I have known and the assurance of eternal life that is now mine. Amen.

Good next moves are to get yourself a Bible that is easy to understand and begin to read. Maybe start in John so you can discover all about Jesus for yourself. Start to pray – prayer is simply talking to God – and, finally, find a church that's alive and get your life planted in it. These simple ingredients will cause your relationship with

God to grow.

Why not email us and let us know if you did that so we can rejoice with you? Tell us about your redemption story.

Great Big Life Publishing
info@greatbiglifepublishing.com

FURTHER INFORMATION

For further information about the authors of this book, or to order more copies, please contact:

Great Big Life Publishing
Empower Centre
83-87 Kingston Road
Portsmouth
Hampshire
PO2 7DX
United Kingdom
info@greatbiglifepublishing.com

ARE YOU AN AUTHOR?

Do you have a word from God on your heart that you're looking to get published to a wider audience?

We're looking for manuscripts that identify with our own vision of bringing life-giving and relevant messages to Body of Christ. Send yours for review towards possible publication to:

Great Big Life Publishing
Empower Centre
83-87 Kingston Road
Portsmouth
Hampshire
PO2 7DX
United Kingdom
info@greatbiglifepublishing.com